Faith, Family & Finances

Faith, Family & Finances

Volume One

John Marshall

Faith, Family, and Finances—Volume One
© 2008 by John Marshall

This book or parts thereof may not be reproduced in any form, stored in a retrieval system, or transmitted in any form by any means—electronic, mechanical, photocopy, recording, or otherwise—without prior written permission of the publisher, except as provided by United States of America copyright law.

Copyright © 2008 by John Marshall
All rights reserved

Unless otherwise noted, all Scripture quotations are from the New American Standard Bible. Copyright © 1960, 1962, 1963, 1968, 1971, 1972, 1973, 1975, 1977 by the Lockman Foundation. Used by permission. (www.Lockman.org)

Cover Design and Layout: Cathleen Kwas

ISBN: 978-0-9820475-0-7
2nd Printing
Printed in the United States of America

DEDICATION

More than twenty (20) years ago, God placed a burning desire within my heart to plant a congregation of the Lord's church. In the 80's, I attempted to plant a congregation in Warsaw, North Carolina. But, God said this is neither the time nor the place. In the 90's, I attempted to plant a congregation in Gastonia, North Carolina. Again, God said this is neither the time nor the place. In 2003, that evangelistic fever returned more passionately than ever, therefore, I planned once again to launch out in 2005 and see what God would say this time.

Beginning with four people less than three years ago, God launched the Graceview Church of Christ and has worked great wonders therein. God has grown Graceview to more than 125 members and are among God's most peaceful people. Because God has blessed me to work with His peaceful people, I dedicate this book to Graceview, God's finest.

Lest I am perceived to give a less than balanced report, I must admit that stragglers have occasionally thrown a few lemons our way. God was mindful to catch them for us, add sweetener, and return to us lemonade. Yes, God has changed every negative vibe into a positive vibration. This dedication says to the Graceview saints, "Let the Glory of the Lord rise among us."

CONTENTS

	Dedication	5
Preface	The Realistic God	9

Part 1—Faith

Chapter 1	The Specifics of Faith	21
Chapter 2	The Spectrum of Faith	31
Chapter 3	Faith in the Blank	36
Chapter 4	Faithing Your Fears	45
Chapter 5	Faith Supersize It!	53
Chapter 6	Just Say the Word	58
Chapter 7	Wilderness Experience	62
Chapter 8	Prioritize	68
Chapter 9	Emphasize	71
Chapter 10	Making It on Broken Pieces	74

Part 2—Family

Chapter 11	What's Character Got to Do With It?	81
Chapter 12	A God-Centered Identity	93
Chapter 13	What Is Marriage?	109
Chapter 14	God Recommended Honorable Covenant—For Your Benefit	115

Chapter 15	Looking in the Wrong Places and Finding the Right Person	121
Chapter 16	What Shall I Bring to My Wedding?	125
Chapter 17	Conflict Resolution Within the Marriage Relationship	132
Chapter 18	Single Parenting	136
Chapter 19	Step-Parenting	141

Part 3—Finances

Chapter 20	God's Honorarium—The Portion: Adam	147
Chapter 21	God's Honorarium—The Priority: Abel	152
Chapter 22	God's Honorarium—The Permanence: Abraham	156
Chapter 23	God's Honorarium—The Prosperity: Tithe & Offerings	164
Chapter 24	God's Stewardship—Attitudes and Blessings	170
Chapter 25	God's Stewardship—Contribution and Expectations	176
Chapter 26	God's Stewardship—Watching the Wisdom of a Widow Woman	181
Chapter 27	Family Financial Models	184
	Epilogue	189

Preface

THE REALISTIC GOD

GOD WANTS TO PUT US INTO THE ONE BODY of Christ, *"For by one Spirit we were all baptized into one body, whether Jews or Greeks, whether slaves or free, and we were all made to drink of one Spirit"* (1 Corinthians 12:13). We have been baptized into the one body by the one Spirit.

God Builds

John the Baptist announced that Jesus would baptize with the Holy Spirit (Matthew 3:11; Mark 1:8; Luke 3:16; John 1:33). He made that statement to the general population before Jesus ever began choosing His Apostles. But what did he mean?

By the Holy Spirit, Jesus baptizes us all into the one body of Christ. Persons whom Jesus Himself baptizes by the Holy Spirit are all truly members of His one body, without regard to fleshly, earthly distinctions or barriers (1 Corinthians 12:13; Galatians 3:26-27; Ephesians 2:18).

The baptism work of the Holy Spirit has to do with the body of Christ, the church. By the Spirit baptism, we are immersed into the body of Christ. Here the Spirit is the instrument, the agent, who places the believer into the body of Christ.

> The creation of the one body is the result of the baptism work of the Holy Spirit.

The creation of the one body is the result of the baptism work of the Holy Spirit. At the moment of salvation, the baptism work of the Holy Spirit inducts the believer as a living member into the body of Christ.

We who are baptized by the Holy Spirit may continue to draw refreshment and spiritual nourishment from that same inexhaustible source (John 4:13-14; 7:37-39). For example, the wedding ceremony inducts a man and a woman into the union of husband and wife. The moment the officiary visibly and verbally pronounces the two as husband and wife, the state invisibly and nonverbally pronounces the two as husband and wife as well. Likewise, the baptism of a candidate inducts him/her into a union within the body of Christ. The moment the performer (baptizer) visibly and verbally baptizes a believer in water, the Holy Spirit invisibly and nonverbally baptizes that person into the body of Christ.

God places us within the body as He so desires. He places one as the hand to perform one function, while He places another as the eye to perform a different function.

Has the Holy Spirit placed (baptized) you into the one body? Has the Holy Spirit placed you into the body where you are? Are you where God placed you? Are you sure you are where God has placed you?

God Causes

The gospel to the Romans, written by the apostle Paul, provides gracious insights into the mind of God. Chapter seven ended with the agony of the believer (Romans 7:14-23), while chapter eight began with the assurance of the believer. Chapter eight ended with the security of the believer (Romans 8:26-39) while it began with the sonship of the believer (Romans 8:1-25). It also ended with no separation for the believer (Romans 8:35-37), while it began with no condemnation for the believer (Romans 8:1).

In chapter one through seven the author mentions the Holy Spirit only once, but in chapter eight he mentions the Holy Spirit twenty times. The Holy Spirit, a new resident, comes to live within the believer and provides a new nature, which in turn produces a new mind. Therefore, the author argues that the Holy Spirit empowers believers to live victoriously even in the flesh.

God guarantees our successful existence within this new life. He assures our successful existence by causing all things to work together: *"And we know that God causes all things to work together for good to those who love God, to those who are called according to His purpose"* (Romans 8:28). What things does God cause to work together?

 God causes all things that the Holy Spirit does to work.

God causes all things that the Holy Spirit does to work. Carefully read the other verses in this chapter. They argue this fact (Romans 8:2, 9, 11, 14, 16, 26-27, 32).

God causes all things that the Holy Spirit does to work together (Romans 8:28). The original term translated "work together" (synergeō) is closely linked to our English word "synergy". Synergy refers to a product or effect resulting from the interaction of items or ingredients that are greater than the sum total.

God causes all things to work together for good. What good? Sometimes all things work together for ultimate good, but not immediate good. Ultimately it was good for Joseph to reside in Egypt, but it certainly did not seem to be immediately good (Genesis 50:20). Sometimes all things work together for collective good, but not for individual good. The crucifixion of Jesus was collectively good for all of us, but not necessarily individually good for Jesus (Matthew 26:36-39).

God causes all things to work together for good to those who love God, and to those who are called according to His purpose. God causes all things to work together for good for those who are active—"love God." God causes all things to work together for good for those who are acted upon—"called according to His purpose."

God has called you that He might place you within your set place. Yes, indeed, God guarantees your successful existence in this new life.

The Real Jesus

Communicating with Jesus only when we have a crisis in our lives limits our relationship with Him. We become preoccupied with getting the Lord to help us with our plans rather than hearing His exciting plans for us.

Jesus wants to show us a life that is far greater than anything we have ever imagined. Often though, He must first speak hard words to wake us up. He positions these difficult sayings throughout scripture, many of which we tend to skip over in search of teachings that appeal to us.

Nevertheless, Jesus presents soul-sized challenges along with His offer to help us accomplish them. He may even confront us with challenges that require far greater power from Him than we have ever experienced. He does this to make us victorious beyond our wildest imagination.

While ministering during His earthly pilgrimage, Jesus uttered some sayings that were hard to interpret and others that were hard to incorporate into life. Often, we prefer to believe that we can omit His hard sayings as if they provide no benefit at all. Nevertheless, these hard sayings of Jesus offer the very secrets of how to put Him first in our lives and begin to realize our full potential. They make up the training manual for a real Jesus Christ-empowered religion.

Jesus multiplied five barley loaves of bread and a few pieces of fish in order to fed 5,000 people. But more than filling their empty stomachs, Jesus wanted to satisfy the deeper hunger and thirst lingering in their hearts. He claimed to be "the bread of life" that came down from heaven and could eternally satisfy their hunger and thirst.

In Jesus' day, when people had worked to the point of exhaustion, they often said, "I have eaten my body and drunk my blood." In other words, they had given themselves completely to their task. Therefore, when a leader called for the unreserved commitment of his followers, he demanded that they "eat his flesh and drink his blood." This was a colorful metaphor indicating total loyalty and allegiance.

When Jesus uttered this "hard" saying about eating His flesh and drinking His blood, "the real Jesus" was inviting His disciples to a communion and a commitment with Him (John 6:53-56). Those who first heard His saying strongly objected, not because they misunderstood, but because they understood all too well what He meant. They knew that He was calling them to accept Him as the Son of God. They knew that He was calling them to concretely commit and constantly commune with Him.

 For their commitment, Jesus promised to satisfy all of their spiritual hungers and thirsts.

For their commitment, Jesus promised to satisfy all of their spiritual hungers and thirsts. Would not everyone readily participate in this kind of relationship? Surprisingly enough, those who first heard Jesus rejected His invitation. They refused to comply with the requirements of this kind of relationship. How willing are you to do differently?

For many, life is just one big struggle. Even some Christians just struggle to keep struggling. Satan has deceived them into believing that life has nothing more to offer than continual struggles.

Whereas all Christians may believe in Jesus, all have not committed their lives totally to Him. When Jesus said, *"... Eat the flesh of the Son of Man and drink his blood..."* (John 6:53), He was soliciting a complete surrender of our minds, emotions, and wills.

The Hebrew word for "flesh" means humanity, so Jesus was referring to His incarnation. We can satisfy our spiritual hunger by feasting upon this fact: That Jesus, full of grace and truth as God's ultimate word, dwelt among us. Digesting this nourishment empowers us far beyond our struggle.

Hopefully, the spiritual nourishments and nuggets within Faith, Family, and Finances will help you to allow God to lead you along the path that His Son Jesus has marched. Now Take. Read.

God has always worked to instill faith within His people. After instilling faith within His people, God took upon Himself the task of rebuilding faith within His people. For God, enabling His people to walk by faith is Job 1.

Faith is the law of God (Romans 3:27-31). Also, faith is the nature of God (2 Peter 1:1). Therefore, when we walk in faith, we are behaving as much like God as we will ever behave. When we fail to walk by faith, we are behaving as much unlike God as we will ever behave. Yes, determines the quality of the believer's life and lifestyle.

PART I

FAITH

Chapter 1

THE SPECIFICS OF FAITH

"And without faith it is impossible to please Him, for he who comes to God must believe that He is and that He is a rewarder of those who seek Him."
— Hebrews 11:6

USING THE SCRIPTURE WHICH SAYS, "...WITHOUT *faith it is impossible to please Him,"* God informs believers of the essential importance of faith (Hebrews 11:6a). Scripture never says, "without money it is impossible to please Him." As essential as love is, scripture never says that without love it is impossible to please God.

Lack of faith is the only thing that God says makes it impossible to please Him. From faith flows our healthy obedience to the call and command of God. With faith, it is possible to please God.

For example, without oxygen, it is impossible for humans to breathe. With oxygen, it is possible for humans to breathe. Faith is the oxygen which sustains our spiritual life. Indeed, God wants believers to function according to faith.

Faith is what we instrumentally do about what we intellectually (illuminative, inspirationally) believe that God has approved (2 Corinthians 4:13, John 7:38). Those saints who are listed in the "Hall of Faith" did what they believed God had approved (Hebrews 11:4, 7, 8, 9, 10, 17). Likewise, God approves it, we believe it and then we act upon it.

If God approves it, but I do not believe it, there is no faith. If God approves it and I believe it, but refuse to act accordingly, there is no faith. Faith is what I instrumentally do about what I intellectually believe that God approves.

We need a functional understanding of faith, which is more valuable than a rote recollection of memorized facts. For example, I can read and memorize the recipe for a German Chocolate Cake. Yet, I have no understanding of how to combine the ingredients in such a manner as to produce an edible product. However, those with a functional understanding of the recipe can mix the ingredients in such a manner to please the palate of all who will indulge. Likewise, a functional understanding of faith relates the components of faith in such a way as to produce a spiritual outcome.

THE SPECIFICS OF FAITH

WHAT ARE THE COMPONENTS OF FAITH?

There must be an *object* for our faith, "Some One" or "Some Thing" toward whom we direct our faith. God, Himself, decided that He would be the object of our faith (Hebrews 11:6b, Exodus 20:1-6, John 6:44-45). The divine record begins by declaring the existence of God, *"In the beginning God…"* (Genesis 1:1). The Ten Commandments denounce and deny all other gods except Jehovah God, *"I am the Lord your God, who brought you out of the land of Egypt, out of the house of slavery. You shall have no other gods before Me"* (Exodus 20:2-3).

We are only as capable as the object of our faith (1 Timothy 6:17-19; Matthew 6:5; 1 Samuel 17:43). The prophets of Baal were only as capable as their god, Baal (1 Kings 18:20-29), which existed only within the minds of the worshipers. Baal, a false god, was powerless to do anything for its worshipers. Therefore, the weakness of their god reduced the power of the worshippers to zero, which rendered them powerless. Thus, the powerlessness of Baal created undue anxiety within them.

We can grow in the capabilities of the object for our faith, but we can never exceed them. The prophet Elijah was as capable as was Jehovah, his God (1 Kings 18:30-39). Likewise, we are as capable as the object of our faith (Hebrews 11:11; Matthew 6:6).

Faith is what you do about what you believe that God approves.

Therefore, we must develop a functional understanding of faith. Remember that faith is not just what you believe; faith is an action word (John 20:27). Faith is what you do about what you believe that God approves. You can become only as capable as your faithfulness to the object of your faith. However, lack of faithfulness to the object of your faith limits your capabilities.

In addition to the object of our faith, there is an **opportunity** for our faith. There must be some expectation for favorable circumstances and/or outcome. God designed His faith to bring about favorable opportunities and outcomes for His people.

God decided that He would reward our faith (Hebrews 11:6c; Genesis 15:18; Revelation 12:12) therefore, we have a right to expect God to do so. Jesus had just completed an encounter with a rich young ruler during which He told the young man to sell what he had and give to the poor (Matthew 19:16-22). Immediately thereafter, one of Jesus' hand-selected apostles, Peter, declared that they had exercised faith and left everything to follow Jesus and he wanted to know what their reward would be. Jesus did not rebuke him for being selfish, but instead told Peter what their reward would be (vv 27-29).

Some people believe that we should serve God just to receive eternal life. Jesus told Peter and the disciples that for

THE SPECIFICS OF FAITH

their faithful service, they would receive more than eternal life. He said that they would receive many times over what they had given up, and in addition, would also inherit eternal life.

God operates in the multiplying business. You are wise to do "faith" business with God, because you have a right to expect God to reward your faith.

Not only do we have a right to expect God to reward our faith, we have a responsibility to believe that God will reward our faith, *"...for he who comes to God must believe that He is a rewarder...."* Notice the little word *"must"*. What happens to the person who does not believe that God will reward? That person fails to receive. God wants to reward, but He withholds it because of the person's lack of belief.

God wants to give generously. However, we must believe—exercise faith—in order to receive (James 1:5-7). We must ask in faith with no doubt that we will receive. If we doubt, we have no right to expect to receive from God. We have no right, because we have no faith to receive.

Even the devil knows that God rewards His people. Consider this question he asked God, *"... Does Job fear God for nothing? Have You not made a hedge about him and his house and all that he has, on every side? You have blessed the work of his hands, and his possessions have increased in the land"* (Job 1:9-10). Satan knew that God had rewarded Job for his faithfulness.

So, who took Job's stuff? The devil took it. Who gave Job back his stuff? God gave it back to him. In fact, the latter part of Job's life was more prosperous because God gave him more than He had given him earlier, *"…the Lord blessed the latter days of Job more than his beginning…"* (Job 42:12).

The devil knows that God rewards our faith, but he wants to keep us from knowing it. Many believers miss the blessings of God because they are unaware of His promises. They are unaware and do not believe that He will reward. Therefore, because they do not believe, God withholds.

How sad it is to be ignorant of God's Word. Aren't you glad that you are becoming enlightened? Are you happy enough to tell others?

I attended Jackson State Community College during 1977-1978. Upon registering each quarter, I wrote a check for the full tuition. After completing 90 hours of course work, the Director of Admission informed me that I had been eligible for a full academic scholarship from the beginning and asked me why I had not applied for it. Unfortunately, I had not taken the time to read the catalog so I did not know that I was eligible for an academic scholarship. The paid tuition had been an unnecessary expense.

Why did the college not give me the scholarship? They withheld the funds because I did not believe to ask, not because they wanted to withhold them. I did not believe to ask because I did not know to ask. I did not know because I had not taken the time to read and learn. Therefore, I failed to receive because I did not believe.

Worship is an expression of faith, so what do you expect God to do for you as a result of your worship? If God rewards

THE SPECIFICS OF FAITH

faith, and worship is an expression of faith, there should be some favorable response on your behalf from God.

 You have a right to say, "God I have exercised my faith now provide what I need."

What do you need God to do for you? You have a right to say, "God I have exercised my faith, now provide what I need." If you need courage, you have a right to ask for it. If you need favor with your adversaries, you have a right to ask for favor with your adversaries.

I had a right to ask for the scholarship, but only because the school had promised it. Likewise, we have a right to ask of God, but only because He has promised. Therefore, we can come boldly to God asking for our reward, *"...let us draw near with confidence..."* (Hebrews 4:16).

Mr. & Mrs. Henry Brown promised to give to each of their three children $1 for each B and $2 for each A achieved on their academic school report card. For the promised grading period, their children made all C's. Since none of the children made an A or a B, the parents will now be able to keep the money for themselves. But what would you think if you overheard them joyfully proclaiming that their children made all C's, knowing they would not have to pay their children? Did the parents promise the gift because they really wanted to give it, or did they promise it grudgingly hoping that the children would fail and they would not have to give the gift?

Good parents want to reward good (faithful) children. They obtain the greater joy when their children succeed and receive their promised reward. Likewise, our God wants to reward His faithful children. He gets greater joy when His children succeed and receive His reward. Therefore, it is neither a strain nor a drain upon God to reward His faithful children.

God has made promises to us. If we do not believe that He will honor His promises, then He will not. God will withhold His favorable response toward us, not because He doesn't want to favor us, but because we do not believe that He will favor us. We have a responsibility to expect God to reward our faith, not because of our faith, but because of His promise to reward our faith.

In addition to there being an object and an opportunity for our faith, there is also an ***obligation*** for our faith. God, Himself, decided that He would demand something from our faith (Hebrews 11:6d). Not only do we have a right to seek God, we have a responsibility to seek God.

What does it mean to seek God? Some have never begun to seek God, so for them to seek God is to begin obeying the word of the Lord.

Scripture records a time when the Israelites had been without a teacher, *"For many days Israel was without the true God and without a teaching priest and without law"* (2 Chronicles 15:3). Being without a teacher, they were without knowledge of the word. Being without knowledge of the word, they had not obeyed the word. Being without obedience to the word caused Azariah, the man of God, to charge Israel to seek God, *"...And if you seek Him, He will let you find Him..."* (2 Chronicles 15:2). Having not obeyed the word, they had stifled their obedience (2 Chronicles 15:1-7; 1 Chronicles 28:8-10).

Some have begun to seek God and are continuing to do so. For them, to seek God is to continue obeying the word of the Lord, *"... He did right in the sight of the Lord according to all that his father Amaziah had done. He continued to seek God in the days of Zechariah..."* (2 Chronicles 26:1-5). Verse four tells us that Uzziah did right. To do right is to follow the commands of God. Verse five tells us that he continued to seek God. How did he seek God? He sought God by continuing to do right and obeying the commands of God.

Some had begun to seek God but have ceased to do so. For them, to seek God is to return to obeying the word of the Lord (Deuteronomy 4:25-31; Isaiah 55:6-13; Daniel 9:1-6). Initially, the priests had begun to serve God but had ceased carrying the ark as they had been instructed (1 Chronicles 15:11-15). King David reminded them of their negligence which had brought the wrath of God upon them. He defined their negligence as a failure to seek God. Fortunately, they returned to seeing God and following His commandments.

Make up your mind to seek God. When you do so, you can expect His reconciliation and His resources. He has promised to reward those who seek Him, *"And without faith it is impossible to please Him, for he who comes to God must believe that He is, and that He is a rewarder of those who seek Him"* (Hebrews 11:6). How vigorously are you seeking God?

Faith is not just what you believe; faith is an action word (John 20:27). Faith is your response to what you believe God approves of (Hebrews 11:7, 8, 9, 10, 11; 2 Corinthians 4:13). You can become only as capable as your faithfulness to the object of your faith. Lack of faithfulness to the object of your faith limits your capabilities.

The next time a person asks you to pray for God to reward them, ask them this question: "Are you seeking God?" If they are not, there is really no point in praying for God's favor.

Chapter 2

THE SPECTRUM OF FAITH

"And without faith it is impossible to please Him, for he who comes to God must believe that He is and that He is a rewarder of those who seek Him."
— Hebrews 11:6

FAITH TEST FAILURES INDICATE THAT FLAWS EXIST within our faith that must be repaired. Before we can repair flaws in our faith, we must first chart where we are on the spectrum of faith. We need to know where we are in our faith maturation process.

Faith in the Object But Faithlessness in the Opportunity and Obligation

One point on the spectrum of faith is where we believe in the object of faith (God), but disbelieve the opportunity and the obligation of faith. At this point, we believe that God does exist but do not believe that He will do anything of value for us. Therefore, we refuse to honor and obey Him. Yes, we have faith in the object of faith, but no faith (fear) in the opportunity or in the obligation of faith.

The children of Israel were at this point (Malachi 3:8-12). They believed in God, the object of faith...no doubt existed in their minds that God did exist. Yet, they refused to believe that the Lord would bless them (opportunity). Because they did not believe the Lord would bless them, they refused to behave according to His guidance (obligation). God had requested tithes from His people long before, but eventually they refused to obey. Why did they refuse to tithe? They did not tithe because they did not believe that God would pour out for them a blessing from heaven. Therefore, God challenged them to tithe to see how He would abundantly bless them (Malachi 3:10-11).

The rich young ruler was at this point as well (Luke 18:18-30). He believed in God, the object of faith. He also believed that eternal life was available and that Jesus was a good master. No doubt existed in his mind that God did exist, yet he refused to believe that the Lord would bless him (opportunity). Jesus commanded the ruler to sell all he had and give it to the poor. Eternal life would be granted to him upon honoring the Lord's request. However, because he did not believe that the Lord would bless him, he refused to behave according to Jesus' guidance (obligation). He, therefore, refused to sell what he had and give it to the poor.

Both the children of Israel and the rich ruler refused to believe in the opportunity of faith. They refused to believe the promises and provisions of faith. Therefore, they refused to behave according to the obligation of faith. They refused to behave according to the principles and procedures of faith.

Likewise, we often vacillate from one area to another from one time to another [Genesis 6:22; Hebrews 11:7]. When we don't believe that a favorable reciprocal response is forthcoming from God, we are unlikely to respond favorably toward His commandments. An unwillingness to obey God, the object of our faith, is symptomatic of a flawed, unhealthy faith. We believe in God, but refuse to love our enemies and do good toward them as He commands because we believe that nothing good will be forthcoming.

Faith in the Object and the Obligation But Faithlessness in the Opportunity

Another point on the spectrum of faith is where we believe in the object of faith (God) and the obligation of faith, while disbelieving in the opportunity of faith. At this point, we believe that God does exist and that we ought to obey Him; yet, we refuse to believe that He will adequately reward us. Yes, we have faith in the object and obligation but no faith (fear) in the opportunity. We believe and behave but say we do not believe that anything will happen.

Zachariah was at this point. He behaved according to the obligation of faith and prayed for a son (Luke 1:5-17), but he did not believe the opportunity of faith (Luke 1:18-20). He walked blamelessly according to God's guidance and prayed for a son, but did not believe that God would honor His request.

The church was even at this point (Acts 12:1-5). They behaved according to the obligation of faith and prayed for Peter's release from prison, but they did not believe the opportunity of faith (Acts 12:6-17). The church prayed for Peter's release but had difficulty believing that God would move on their behalf. Traditional and habitual worshippers often engage in worship, yet never believe they will receive anything from their engagement.

Both Zachariah and the church behaved according to the obligation of faith, yet they refused to believe in the opportunity of faith. They behaved according to the principles and procedures of faith while not believing in the promises and provisions of faith.

Faith in the Object and the Opportunity but Faithlessness in the Obligation

An additional point on the spectrum of faith is where we believe in the object and the opportunity while disbelieving in the obligation. At this point, we believe that God does exist and that He will reward us, yet we refuse to behave according to the obligation of faith. We have faith in the object and the opportunity, but no faith (fear) in the obligation.

Naaman was at this point (2 Kings 5:1-9). He believed in the opportunity of faith and went to the king and the prophet. Yet, initially, he did not behave according to the obligation of faith (2 Kings 5:10-12). Fortunately, he subsequently did behave according to the obligation of faith and went into the Jordan River and dipped seven times as the man of God had instructed (2 Kings 5:13-14). Being faithful to the obligation of faith resulted in Naaman being completely cleansed of leprosy.

The Hebrews were at this point as well (Romans 10:1-3). They believed in God and desired His salvation while neglecting to obey His righteous requests.

Both Naaman and the Hebrews believed according to the opportunity of faith, but refused to behave according to the obligation of faith. They expected the promises and provisions of faith without obeying the principles and procedures for faith.

Chapter 3

FAITH IN THE BLANK

> *"Now there was a famine in the land; so Abram went down to Egypt to sojourn there, for the famine was severe in the land."*
>
> —Genesis 12:10

THROUGH ABRAM, GOD CREATED THE HEBREW race that would give birth to Jesus Christ, the son of God. Therefore, God chose Abram to illustrate the salvation that He would later provide in Christ Jesus. Abram would *visibly* illustrate the salvation that God would *invisibly* provide.

Time and time again after choosing Abram, God tested his faith. Time and time again Abram failed miserably his faith test. On this occasion (a famine in the land), Abram failed the faith test.

Frequently, God tests our faith. Unfortunately, we, like Abram, often fail.

How Do We Fail Our Faith Test?

We fail our faith test when we leave the place God has led us. God had led Abram to Canaan (Genesis 11:31), but he left Canaan and went down into Egypt because of the famine (Genesis 12:10). God had told Abram to go to the land that God would show him (Genesis 12:1), and He showed (led) him to the land of Canaan (Genesis 12:5). We see no indication in scripture that God ever led Abram to Egypt.

Canaan was a type of the church and heaven. Though a famine came into the land, God still had plans to nourish Abram there (Genesis 12:2-3). No matter what the circumstances, God was fully capable of blessing Abram in Canaan. Nevertheless, irritations came even though Abram was in the place where God had led him and wanted him to be. Be aware of this: Irritations are often a part of the test and do not always indicate that one is outside of the will of God.

Egypt was a type of the world and hell. God had not planned to nourish Abram in Egypt, even though he enjoyed a degree of economic prosperity there (Genesis 12:16). Prosperity does not always mean that we are within the will of God.

Because Abram left the place where God led him, he lost his peace and security (Genesis 12:11-12). In essence, Abram left heaven and went to hell. He left the church and went back into the world. He trusted God to lead him to Canaan, but did not trust God to sustain him there. Peace and security are more of an indicator of the favor of God than economic prosperity.

We constantly leave the peace and security that God provides. It's as if we constantly leave heaven and wander back into hell. And yes, we are ever leaving the church and walking back into the world.

We need to know without a doubt that God is leading us. Only when we apprehend that fact can we begin to know where God is leading us.

WHERE HAS GOD LED YOU?

Where has God led you intellectually? What knowledge and wisdom has God allowed you to apprehend? Has God led you to discover knowledge that will enhance your physical health? Why have you left that knowledge? Why have you walked away from doing that which improves your health? Did you allow something to drive you away or draw you away from what you had learned? Whatever the case, therein, you failed your faith test.

All true knowledge comes from God, and He leads us to and through our knowledge and understanding. He allows us to discover such knowledge for His leading.

We fail our faith test when we deny the person to whom God has wed us. God wed Abram to Sarai, but Abram denied the person to whom God wed him (Genesis 12:11-13).

Sarai was indeed Abram's sister (Genesis 20:11-13), but she was also his wife. What he said was true, "that she was his sister," but what he did was deceitful…Abram allowed Sarai to be positioned as an unmarried woman. Abram led Pharaoh to believe that Sarai was unmarried, thus allowing Pharaoh to behave toward her as if she were unmarried (Genesis 12:14-16).

Abram did not have to tell Pharaoh everything that he asked. Nevertheless, when suppression led to deception, which led to sin, Abram became accountable.

 Even if we fail our faith test, God invites us back into fellowship with Him.

Even if we fail our faith test, God invites us back into fellowship with Him. God allows retakes. No matter how miserably we fail, He invites us back into fellowship without embarrassment.

Whenever little children wander into mud and water after their parents have dressed them all nice and neat, good parents put another set of clean clothes on their children. No matter how muddy their children become, good parents always clean them up and provide clean clothes. God is just like that. No matter how far we wander away, He readily retrieves those who allow Him. The reception granted by the spurned father at the return of his prodigal son demonstrates what God is like (Luke 15:11-32).

He who is least qualified to condemn us usually will condemn. Scripture records how some men had caught a woman in the very act of adultery (John 8:1-11). The Law required that both the man and woman be stoned to death (Leviticus 20:10; Deuteronomy 22:22), but the men released the guilty man and brought the guilty woman to Jesus. They were in violation of the Law themselves and invited Jesus to participate with them in stoning the woman. Though these men were least qualified to condemn her, they were ready and anxious to do so.

He who is most qualified to condemn us usually will not condemn. Jesus had never sinned, neither did He endorse sin in this instance, but instead refused to participate in impartial justice. Challenging the woman to go and sin no more, He raised the standard for her. Jesus was most qualified to condemn her, but He was unwilling to do so.

You may not have failed your last faith test, but when you fail, God will quickly welcome you back into fellowship. He does not rejoice in your failure, but rather provides reinforcement so that you will succeed (1 John 2:1).

Unfortunately, human frailty overshadows us. These stories of human failure and subsequent success give us hope. If Abram can fail, recover and then become listed within the "hall of faith," hope exists for us (Hebrews 11:8ff).

How Can We Pass Our Faith Test?

In order to pass our faith test, we must refuse to become fear-driven and instead remain faith-led. Faith and fear are opposites, so people who are driven by fear usually fail their faith test.

Abram became fear-driven (Genesis 12:11-13). His unwarranted fear of the Egyptians drove Abram to mislead Pharaoh to believe that Sarai, his wife, was unmarried. Likewise, our unwarranted fear will cause us to fail our faith test.

Abram could have remained faith-led if he had kept telling himself what God had said instead of saying what he thought the Egyptians would do (Genesis 12:1-3). We must keep telling ourselves what God says: "...for He Himself has said, 'I WILL NEVER DESERT YOU, NOR WILL I EVER FORSAKE YOU'" (Hebrews 13:5).

God said, *"I will never desert you"*. To desert means "to cease to support or sustain, let sink and drown." God also said, *"nor will I ever forsake you."* To forsake is to "let down when hostile circumstances are against you, abandon when the enemy approaches, retreat, and leave you to do battle alone" (2 Timothy 4:10-16; 2 Samuel 11:14-17).

What troubling circumstances are you facing? God says, "I am with you so that you can speak confidently—to be of good cheer, have courage, be full of hope and confidence" (Hebrews 13:6; 2 Corinthians 5:6-8).

Always reject the notion that God provides for eternal things while neglecting earthly things. God created us to need earthly, temporary things and He delights in providing them for us. People who trust God for eternal things, but refuse to trust him for earthly things will usually fail their faith test.

Abram trusted God to provide for long term commitment, but failed to trust for his immediate needs (Genesis 12:10). We must trust God for our earthly needs (Luke 12:22-31).

Jesus said we can trust God to provide for our food. He provides for the fowls and Jesus said that we are more valuable than they (Luke 12:24). What father would feed his chickens but starve his children? We can also trust Him to provide for our fashion (covering). He provides fashion for the flowers of the field and again, Jesus said we are more valuable than they (Luke 12:27-28). It is God who keeps us. We cannot keep ourselves. Trust God regardless.

How Can We Recover From Our Faith Test Failure?

In order to recover from our faith test failures, we must renew our fellowship with God. Abram renewed his fellowship with God; we must do the same. How do we renew our fellowship with God?

Prioritize our worship, expressions of allegiance and appreciation to God. Abram returned to Bethel, the place where he had earlier built an altar and called upon the name of the Lord (Genesis 12:7-8; 13:3-4, 18). Neither in Haran nor in Egypt is there any mention of his fellowship with God, no mention of building altars and there is no mention of him calling upon the name of the Lord (Genesis 11:31; 12:10-13:1).

Glamorize our witness [testimony]. Abram wanted the heathens [Canaanites and Perizzites] to see harmony between brothers (Genesis 13:6-8). Therefore, he concerned himself with how they looked even to the heathens.

Realize that renewal of fellowship often leaves a residual effect of sin. Abram renewed his fellowship with God, but continually experienced irritations.

Realize that what you bring with you from the world [Egypt] into the church [Canaan] may continually irritate you. To Canaan, Abram brought with him sheep and cattle out of Egypt (Genesis 12:16; 13:1-2). There is a significant difference in the grazing ability of sheep and cattle. Sheep have top and bottom, front and back teeth so they can bite grass very close to the earth. They can also eat twigs. Cattle have no top front teeth so they cannot bite grass close to the earth, it must be long enough for them to twist their tongue around and crop it off. Because of this, cattle are unable to graze where sheep have been.

Realize that who you bring with you from the world [Egypt] into the church [Canaan] may continually irritate you. Abram brought his nephew, Lot, even though God had told him to leave his relatives (Genesis 12:1-3). Then, because Lot had pitched his tent toward Sodom, Abram had to send soldiers to rescue him (Genesis 14:1-16).

Had it not been for Lot, no strife would have erupted. Had it not been for cattle, no strife would have erupted.

God never gives up on His people. We are eternally secure because God is able to keep us (1 Peter 1:5; 2 Peter 2:9; Luke 22:54-60; Galatians 2:11).

God disciplines His people toward recovery as long as His faith remains with them (Hebrews 12:5-11). On our way up, God welcomes our worship regardless of how far down we may have fallen. King David, an adulterous murderer, repented, got up, and went to worship (2 Samuel 12:16-20). Worship is our first recovery step. Even on our way up, people need our witness regardless of how far we may have fallen. Our witness is the second recovery step.

Manage what we have with us. Prosperity may be our punishment. God used Abram's prosperity to get him to finally do what He had asked him to do earlier, separate from relatives.

Manage who we have with us. Our people may be our punishment.

Chapter 4

FAITHING YOUR FEARS

"When you are approaching the battle, the priest shall come near and speak to the people. "He shall say to them, 'Hear, O Israel, you are approaching the battle against your enemies today. Do not be fainthearted. Do not be afraid, or panic, or tremble before them.'"
—Deuteronomy 20:2-3

THE WORD "FEAR" IN SCRIPTURE HOLDS MORE than one meaning. The writer of the book of Hebrews used the word "fear" to describe Noah's respect and reverence for God, "*By faith Noah, being warned of God of things not seen as yet, moved with fear…*" (Hebrews 11:7 KJV). In this instance, fear (reverence) was a healthy attribute.

Why Not Increase Your Faith?

Using a form of the word "fear", the writer of the book of Revelation described a paranoia that paralyzed spiritual participation and progress: *"But the **fearful** and unbelieving, and abominable, and murderers, and whoremongers, and sorcerers, and idolaters, and all liars, shall have their part in the lake which burneth with fire and brimstone: which is the second death"* (Revelation 21:8 KJV). In this instance, fear (paranoia) was an unhealthy attribute.

The Holy Spirit warns us about the tragedy of this paranoia type of fear. Unfortunately, it continues to terrorize many Christians as they have become fearful to the point of being hindered in their spiritual participation and progress. Yet, God never intended for us to be terrorized by fear. Therefore, through His revealed word He thoroughly informed us about fear.

Have you been fearful lately? What does God say about fear? Why do you feel so powerless? Why do you feel fearful so often?

Fear is associated with the idea of control and it surfaces when we feel as if we have lost control. In fact, a "perceived" lack of control causes as much fear as a "real" lack of control.

Perceptions of powerlessness generate fear. However, faithful disciples of Christ are never powerless. The apostle Paul declared, *"I can do all things through Christ which strengtheneth me"* (Philippians 4:13 KJV).

God gives us an *inherent* power because **we are in Him,** *"And what is the exceeding greatness of his power to us-ward who believe…* (Ephesians 1:19-23 KJV). He also gives us an *internal* power because **He is in us,** *". . . according to the power that worketh in us* (Ephesians 3:20 KJV).

*"For God hath not given us a spirit of **fear**, but of power, and of love, and of a sound mind"* (2 Timothy 1:7 KJV). The devil, not God, is the source of our unwholesome fears (paranoia). Now that we know the source of our fears, we can increase our wholesome (reverence) fears and decrease our unwholesome (paranoia) fears.

Why Not Decrease Your Fear?

For it is just like a man about to go on a journey, who called his own slaves, and entrusted his possessions to them. And to one he gave five talents, to another, two, and to another, one, each according to his own ability; and he went on his journey. Immediately the one who had received the five talents went and traded with them, and gained five more talents. In the same manner the one who had received the two talents gained two more. But he who received the one talent went away and dug in the ground, and hid his master's money.

Now after a long time the master of those slaves came and settled accounts with them. And the one who had received the five talents came up and brought five more talents, saying, 'Master, you entrusted five talents to me; see, I have gained five more talents.' His master said to

him, 'Well done, good and faithful slave; you were faithful with a few things, I will put you in charge of many things, enter into the joy of your master.' The one also who had received the two talents came up and said, 'Master, you entrusted to me two talents; see, I have gained two more talents.' His master said to him, 'Well done, good and faithful slave; you were faithful with a few things, I will put you in charge of many things; enter into the joy of your master.' And the one also who had received the one talent came up and said, 'Master, I knew you to be a hard man, reaping where you did not sow, and gathering where you scattered no seed. And I was afraid, and went away and hid your talent in the ground; see, you have what is yours.' But his master answered and said to him, 'You wicked, lazy slave, you knew that I reap where I did not sow, and gather where I scattered no seed. Then you ought to have put my money in the bank, and on my arrival I would have received my money back with interest. Therefore take away the talent from him, and give it to the one who has the ten talents.' For to everyone who has shall more be given, and he shall have an abundance; but from the one who does not have, even what he does have shall be taken away. And cast out the worthless slave into the outer darkness; in that place there shall be weeping and gnashing of teeth.
—Matthew 25:14-30

Initially, the servant who had received just one talent began to make excuses. He argued that a character flaw existed within his lord. However, the fear that existed within the slave was the real problem. Because he was afraid, he hid his lord's money in the ground. With the money hidden, the servant had produced nothing. At the settling of accounts, he presented nothing because he had produced nothing. In the eyes of his lord, the slave was worthless. Likewise, fear causes us to become "worthless" in our own eyes.

What has fear kept you from producing and presenting? You must understand that fear causes you to believe that you are worthless. Knowing this will help you to regain your sense of worth.

Fear, Fear and More Fears

For many, fear is an everyday malady of affliction. What is the remedy for fear? Who or what can save us from this paranoia?

Faith in God is the only remedy for our fears.

Through observing the events of one day in the life of Jesus and His disciples, we can learn much about faith and fear. The writers of the synoptic Gospels, Matthew (Matthew 8:23-27), Mark (Mark 4:35-41), and Luke (Luke 8:22-25) each described the events of that particular day.

Jesus and the disciples had set sail across the Sea of Galilee. While they were underway, Jesus went to sleep on some cushions. Before the boat reached the opposite shore, a savage storm swooped down upon them. As the wind lashed the boat, water came over the side and began to fill the boat.

As the disciples evaluated their situation, they obviously concluded that it was threatening. Then as they evaluated their available resources the men perceived that what they had available was inadequate. This perception of inadequacy caused them to believe that they had lost control. Their sense of having lost control in their environment triggered their emotion of fear.

Abruptly, they awakened Jesus and fearfully exclaimed, (1) *"We are perishing"* (Luke 8:24), (2) *"Teacher, do you not care that we are perishing"* (Mark 4:38), and (3) *"Save us, Lord; we are perishing"* (Matthew 8:25).

Jesus rebuked the wind, calmed the raging sea and then asked His disciples, *"Why are you so timid? How is it that you have no faith"* (Mark 4:40). Do you see how Jesus juxtaposed faith and fear? Faith and fear can never reside simultaneously in the same heart. As fear enters, faith exits. As fear becomes strong, faith becomes weak. As fear increases, faith decreases.

 As faith enters, fear exits. As faith becomes strong, fear becomes weak.

The opposite is also true. As faith enters, fear exits. As faith becomes strong, fear becomes weak. As faith increases, fear decreases. Indeed, faith is the answer to the problem of fear. Faith can save us from the paranoia of fear.

Through His Spirit, God gives us power (Ephesians 1:19-23) and through Christ, He strengthens us (Philippians 4:13). But fear pollutes, dilutes, and destroys our accurate assessment of our potential. Fear confuses our purpose and controls our power. It terrorizes and paralyzes our minds. Fear places us within a preconceived prison and numbers us among the frozen chosen. It infects us with the sadness of analysis paralysis.

More Faith and Less Fear

Faith and fear can never reside simultaneously within the same heart. Faith is the universal remedy that destroys fear.

What is faith?

"But having the same spirit of faith, according to what is written, 'I believed, therefore I spoke,' we also believe, therefore also we speak" (2 Corinthians 4:13). When evidence causes beliefs and those beliefs cause actions, faith results. Faith is the human reaction to God's action.

The saints in the city of Corinth had come to possess the same faith in God as had the apostle Paul. Likewise, we can come to possess that same faith.

The apostle Paul observed the evidence and believed, for he said, *"I believed..."* (v. 13). The saints in Corinth had also observed the evidence and believed. God expects us to believe as well, but only that for which He has provided evidence.

The apostles and prophets wrote the record of God's revelation to humankind (Ephesians 3:1-6). The Bible contains that written record, so it contains the revealed and written record of the evidence upon which our faith in God must be established.

Our faith in God is established upon the revealed, written word of God, *"So faith comes from hearing, and hearing by the word of Christ"* (Romans 10:17). The apostle Paul acknowledged that faith was *"according to what is written"* (2 Corinthians 4:13). Separate and apart from believing valid evidence, faith in God does not exist.

Not only does faith in God depend upon our beliefs, but faith in God demands that we behave. Paul's beliefs caused him to speak and the Corinthians' beliefs caused them to speak, resulting in faith in God (2 Corinthians 4:13). When belief combines with behavior, faith is the end result.

Faith in God is not…

- <u>Just</u> what you believe.
- Just what you believe that the Bible <u>might</u> say.
- Just what you believe that the Bible <u>does</u> say.

Faith in God is…

- What you <u>do</u> about what you believe that the Bible <u>does</u> say (2 Corinthians 4:13; Hebrews 11:6-8).

Therefore, we should:

- Search the scriptures and draw valid conclusions from the evidence.
- Believe only, but believe all of the scripturally valid conclusions.
- Behave according to all of, but only the scripturally valid conclusions.

Chapter 5

FAITH SUPERSIZE IT!

The apostles said to the Lord, "Increase our faith!"
—Luke 17:5

JESUS OFTEN ENGAGED HIS DISCIPLES IN THE CONTEXT of everyday events and then later attached eternal principles to what transpired. However, in the instance discussed below, Jesus reversed that order and taught the eternal real-life principle first and then attached the everyday real-life practice. Therefore, He attached the experience practice of Luke 7:1-10 to the teaching principle in Luke 6:46-49.

Jesus used this event to teach the concept of the "authority of the spoken word." He had said that if one were going to call Him "Lord" then they must do what He says to do (Luke

6:46). By doing what the Lord says, you provide a solid foundation for life (Luke 6:47-49). The instructions you follow today determines the quality of life you will enjoy tomorrow.

An influential Roman centurion [the commanding officer of 100 soldiers] had a highly regarded [dear and valuable] slave who was near to death (Luke 6:2). The centurion heard about the ministry of Jesus so he sent some Jewish elders [advocates] to request a healing visit from Jesus (Luke 6:3).

The Jewish elders delivered the message and recommended the request of the centurion to Jesus (Luke 7:4-5). However, before Jesus arrived, the centurion declared his unworthiness for Jesus to enter his house. Instead, he informed Jesus of his own understanding of the authority of the spoken word (Luke 7:6-7). The centurion understood the authority of the spoken word (Luke 7:8) because he lived a lifestyle of obeying the authoritative spoken word of others. Likewise, others obeyed his authoritative spoken word.

Jesus marveled at the faith of the centurion (Luke 7:9). Interestingly, the gospels record only twice that Jesus marveled at faith. On this occasion, He marveled at the presence of faith and on another occasion, He marveled at the absence of faith (Mark 6:6).

 What the centurion called authority, Jesus called faith.

What the centurion called authority, Jesus called faith. Our response to authority dictates the quality of our faith.

How is this so?

Obeying the authority under which we have been placed indicates the quality of our faith. Jesus equated obeying authority with possessing great faith, *"For I also am a man placed under authority, ... Now when Jesus heard this, He marveled at him, and turned and said to the crowd that was following Him, 'I say to you, not even in Israel have I found such great faith'"* (Luke 7:8-9).

- Obeying the authority under which we are placed within the home is how we develop and exercise authority toward God.

- Obeying the authority under which we are placed within the church is how we develop and exercise faith toward God.

- Obeying the authority under which we are placed within society is how we develop and exercise faith toward God.

Exercising the authority over that which we have been placed indicates the quality of our faith. Jesus equated exercising authority with possessing great faith , *"...with soldiers under me; and I say to this one, 'Go!' and he goes, and to another, 'Come!' and he comes, and to my slave, 'Do this!' and he does it." Now when Jesus heard this, He marveled at him, and turned and said to the crowd that was following Him, 'I say to you, not even in Israel have I found such great faith'* (Luke 7:8-9).

- Exercising the authority over that which we are placed within the home is how we develop and exercise faith toward God. God made Abraham to become a great man of faith. God invested Himself within him because He knew that Abraham would command his children and his household (Genesis 18:17-19). By exercising authority within his household, Abraham developed great faith.

- Exercising the authority over that which we are placed within the church is how we develop and exercise faith toward God. Think it not strange that God required those who would lead within His church to be those who managed their households well, *"He must be one who manages his own household well, keeping his children under control with all dignity (but if a man does not know how to manage his own household, how will he take care of the church of God?)"* (1 Timothy 3:4-5).

- Exercising the authority over that which we are placed within society is how we develop and exercise faith toward God. Joseph dreamed that he would one day exercise authority over his brothers and his parents (Genesis 37:5-10). Exercising authority posed no problem for him and eventually he exercised authority over all of Egypt (Genesis 41:39-57). Because of his willingness to exercise authority over that which he had been placed, Joseph developed great faith.

Chapter 6

JUST SAY THE WORD

Mary said to the angel, "How can this be, since I am a virgin?" The angel answered and said to her, "The Holy Spirit will come upon you, and the power of the Most High will overshadow you; and for that reason the holy Child shall be called the Son of God. And behold, even your relative Elizabeth has also conceived a son in her old age; and she who was called barren is now in her sixth month. For nothing will be impossible with God." And Mary said, "Behold, the bondslave of the Lord; may it be done to me according to your word." And the angel departed from her.

— Luke 1:34-38

THE ANGEL, GABRIEL, INFORMED THE VIRGIN, Mary, that God had chosen her to give birth to Jesus, His Son (Luke 1:26-33). No virgin had ever given birth to a child, so Mary questioned the angel as to how this could be (Luke 1:34).

Humans have come into the world through four different means. God produced Adam without using a man and without using a woman. He just fashioned him from the dust of the earth (Genesis 2:7). But God used both a man and a woman to bring each of us into being. Yes, through the cohabitation of a male and a female, you and I were conceived. God brought Eve into existence by using a man but not using a woman. God extracted a rib from Adam's side and fashioned Eve (Genesis 2:21-23). Finally, God used a woman without using a man to bring Jesus Christ, His begotten Son, into this world. Through His Holy Spirit, Mary was impregnated (Luke 1:35).

Despite the seeming impossibility, Mary believed what God had said about her (Luke 1:35-38). Like Mary, you must condition yourself to totally believe what the word says.

How Can I Condition Myself to Believe?

Say what the word says. Mary began to say what the word said, even before it happened. She extracted a quote from Psalms 34:2ff and began speaking it into existence (Luke 1:46-48). True to God's word, what she said became a reality as she gave birth to Jesus. Her own words became a creative force within her.

Surround yourself with people who will say what the word says. Mary visited Elizabeth, the mother-to-be of John the

Baptist (Luke 1:39-45). When Mary arrived, Elizabeth began speaking the prophecy concerning her. How did Elizabeth know that Mary was going to give birth? She believed the word that Mary had heard and had spoken to her.

Surround yourself with people who will nurture you to say what the word says. Upon hearing Mary's greeting, Elizabeth expressed the same joy as did Mary (Luke 1:41-45). This gracious reception set the foundation for Mary to confidently continue to speak (Luke 1:46ff).

Unfortunately, the contemptible peer pressure of unbelievers has aborted the faith of not just a few believers. You must condition yourself to believe what the word says. God wants you to begin declaring about yourself what the word says about you.

What does the word say about me? The words says that when you are in Christ you are a new creature, *"Therefore if any man is in Christ, he is a new creature; the old things passed away; behold, new things have come"* (2 Corinthians 5:17).

How do I get into Christ? God has reconciled you to Himself, *"Now all these things are from God, who reconciled us to Himself through Christ and gave us the ministry of reconciliation"* (2 Corinthians 5:18). The word "reconcile" expressed the concept of restoring peace. To reconcile means to reestablish a favorable relationship, to transfer from a certain state to another which is quite different and to change the judicial status from condemnation to justification.

When does God reconcile me to Himself? God reconciled you to Himself when He canceled your sin debt, *"namely, that God was in Christ reconciling the world to Himself, not counting their trespasses against them, and He has committed to us the word of reconciliation"* (2 Corinthians 5:19).

How can God dismiss my sin charges against me? God can dismiss the sin charges against you because He has already charged your sins to Christ's account. God made Christ to be sin for you, *"He made Him who knew no sin to be sin on our behalf, so that we might become the righteousness of God in Him"* (2 Corinthians 5:21). Therefore, He who is in Christ is the righteousness of God, not just a poor old sinner.

How do I get into Christ? You are baptized into Christ, *"For you are all sons of God through faith in Christ Jesus. For all of you who were baptized into Christ have clothed yourselves with Christ"* (Galatians 3:26-27). When you become baptized into Christ, you can truthfully and should triumphantly say, "I am the righteousness of God? I am blood-washed. I am no longer sin-stained."

"I am the righteousness of God? I am blood-washed. I am no longer sin-stained."

"I am the righteousness of God? I am blood-washed. I am no longer sin-stained."

Chapter 7

WILDERNESS EXPERIENCE

Jesus, full of the Holy Spirit, returned from the Jordan and was led around by the Spirit in the wilderness for forty days, being tempted by the devil. And He ate nothing during those days, and when they had ended, He became hungry. And the devil said to Him, "If You are the Son of God, tell this stone to become bread." And Jesus answered him, "It is written, 'MAN SHALL NOT LIVE ON BREAD ALONE.'" And he led Him up and showed Him all the kingdoms of the world in a moment of time. And the devil said to Him, "I will give You all this domain and its glory; for it has been handed over to me, and I give it to whomever I wish. Therefore if You worship before me, it shall all be Yours." Jesus answered him, "It is written, 'YOU SHALL WORSHIP THE LORD YOUR GOD AND SERVE HIM ONLY.'" And he led Him to Jerusalem and had Him stand on the pinnacle of the temple, and said to Him, "If You are the Son of God, throw Yourself down from here; for it is written, 'HE WILL COMMAND HIS ANGELS CONCERNING YOU TO GUARD YOU,'" and, 'ON their HANDS THEY WILL BEAR YOU UP, SO THAT YOU WILL NOT STRIKE YOUR FOOT AGAINST A STONE.'" And Jesus answered and said to him, "It is said, 'YOU SHALL NOT PUT THE LORD YOUR GOD TO THE TEST.'" When the devil had finished every temptation, he left Him until an opportune time.

—LUKE 4:1-13

IN THE SPIRIT OF ELIJAH, JOHN, THE SON OF ZACHARIAS and Elizabeth, came preaching and baptizing (Luke 3:1-6). This John baptized Jesus in the Jordan River (Luke 3:21). After Jesus was baptized by John, God publicly crowned Jesus as His beloved Son (Luke 3:22).

Immediately after His public coronation, Jesus entered into His wilderness experience (Luke 4:1). His wilderness included temptations to use His spiritual gifts selfishly (Luke 4:2-11). Fortunately for us, He successfully endured the trials of His time in the wilderness.

After our public coronation, we enter a wilderness experience as well. Our wilderness experience confronts us with critically clear character choices. However, I am delighted to report that God successfully guides us throughout our time of trial and temptation.

What Should I Do While God Guides?

Let's consider the appropriate responses:

Live by every word that proceeds out of the mouth of God **even when all is not well**. Having fasted for forty days, Jesus became hungry (Luke 4:2) so the devil offered him food—a physical temptation (Luke 4:3). Using the word of God, Jesus triumphed over the temptation of the devil, *"And Jesus answered him, 'It is written, 'MAN SHALL NOT LIVE ON BREAD ALONE'"* (Luke 4:4). From where did that notion come? What is its significance?

While the Hebrews wandered in the wilderness, God fed them with manna, a bread-like substance. Though they ate manna, they still died in the wilderness never possessing their promised inheritance. Obviously, bread alone was incapable of sustaining them to live in their inheritance. God reminded them that true life is lived by His word, not by bread alone (Deuteronomy 8:1-20). Upon which do you depend, His word or your bread?

Reverence only the name [authority, character, reputation] of God **when all is very** *well*. The devil offered Jesus "assets with an attitude" in exchange for His worship (Luke 4:5-7). To seek to obtain resources through unapproved means amounts to devil worship. Again, using the word of God, Jesus triumphed over the temptation of the devil, *"Jesus* *answered him, 'It is written, 'YOU SHALL WORSHIP THE LORD YOUR GOD AND SERVE HIM ONLY'''* (Luke 4:8). From where did that notion come? What is its significance?

While the Hebrews wandered in the wilderness, God demanded their exclusive allegiance for Himself. He knew that the idol gods and their worshippers would entice His people, so He warned them of His jealous anger (Deuteronomy 6:10-15; 10:20). Will you worship Jehovah God or will you engage in devil worship?

Trust God to take you from the "not well" stage to the "very well" stage *throughout your life.* The devil invited Jesus to carelessly throw Himself upon the protective care of God (Luke 4:9). He supported the invitation with an invalid application of scripture (Luke 4:10-11) by misapplying what the Psalmist had written (Psalms 91:11-12). For the third time, using the word of God, Jesus triumphed over the temptation of the devil: *"And Jesus answered and said to him, 'It is said, 'YOU SHALL NOT PUT THE LORD YOUR GOD TO THE TEST.'"* (Luke 4:12). From where did that notion come? What is its significance?

While the Hebrews wandered in the wilderness, God provided water from a rock. They drank the water but did not maintain faith in the one who had provided it, so God warned them against testing Him (Deuteronomy 6:16-19; Exodus 17:1-7). Unfortunately, the Hebrews failed to learn their lesson and kept murmuring each time they allowed fear to override their faith.

Observations

- Your wilderness experience *defines* you.

- Your wilderness experience defines and *refines* you.

- Your wilderness experience *defines* your destiny.

- Your wilderness experience defines and *refines* your destiny.

- Your wilderness experience exposes your *workable knowledge of the word of God.*

- Your wilderness experience exposes your *willingness to obey the word of God.*

- God guides those whom He *governs*. Those who cooperate with the Holy Spirit can receive guidance from the word.

- To live *now* during our *wilderness experience,* so that we can live *then* in our *inheritance,* we must digest the word of God.

- God becomes angry when we obtain resources through unapproved means.

WILDERNESS EXPERIENCE

- God has never promised deliverance from selfishly created dangers.

- The devil never leaves until we defeat Him.

- When the devil does leave, he leaves only temporarily awaiting another opportune moment.

- God expects us to defeat the devil with the word, not to depend on angelic help.

God successfully guides us throughout our wilderness experience (Exodus 2:11-4:31) and wants you to welcome yours. Write a paragraph detailing a wilderness experience that helped you to see yourself clearly. Share it with a friend.

Chapter 8

PRIORITIZE

Now as they were traveling along, He entered a village; and a woman named Martha welcomed Him into her home. She had a sister called Mary, who was seated at the Lord's feet, listening to His word. But Martha was distracted with all her preparations; and she came up to Him and said, "Lord, do You not care that my sister has left me to do all the serving alone? Then tell her to help me." But the Lord answered and said to her, "Martha, Martha, you are worried and bothered about so many things; but only one thing is necessary, for Mary has chosen the good part, which shall not be taken away from her."

—Luke 10:38-42

SCENARIO # 1: JESUS VISITED IN MARTHA'S HOME. While Jesus visited in Martha's home, her sister, Mary sat and listened to the word of the Lord. Mary concerned herself with the provisions for the soul.

Scenario # 2: Jesus visited in Martha's home. While Jesus visited in her home, Martha stood and looked after the work of the house. Martha concerned herself with the preparations for the body.

Jesus complimented Mary for prioritizing the provisions of the soul above the preparations for the body. When you prioritize the provisions for the soul over the preparations for the body, God lifts your life to a higher level.

God lifts your life to a higher level because He appreciates you for prioritizing that which is *essential*. God compliments you for placing the one "good" thing above the many "going" things. Mary had chosen the one necessary good part while Martha chose to worry about the many necessary going preparations.

God lifts your life to a higher level because He appreciates you for prioritizing that which is *eternal*. God compliments you for placing the one permanent thing above the many personal things. Mary had chosen to listen to the eternal word while Martha had chosen to look after the earthly work.

When you prioritize the provisions for the soul over the preparations for the body, God lifts your life to a higher level. When God appreciates your choices He appropriates His resources. God wants you to set priorities according to His compliments.

Questions

1. What are your three most urgent agenda items for today and tomorrow?

2. What difference will it make if you accomplish them or not?

3. How many of your urgent agenda items are provisions for the soul?

4. How many of your urgent agenda items are preparations for the body?

Chapter 9

EMPHASIZE

The seventy returned with joy, saying, "Lord, even the demons are subject to us in Your name." And He said to them, "I was watching Satan fall from heaven like lightning. Behold, I have given you authority to tread on serpents and scorpions, and over all the power of the enemy, and nothing will injure you. Nevertheless do not rejoice in this, that the spirits are subject to you, but rejoice that your names are recorded in heaven."
—LUKE 10:17-20

INITIALLY, JESUS CALLED 12 APOSTLES (LUKE 9:1) and then later, He commissioned 70 additional ministry workers (Luke 10:1). Just as He had done for the 12, Jesus gave the 70 authoritative power over the demonic spirits (Luke 10:17-19).

The 70 went out and exercised their authoritative power and then returned with joy over their new found success (Luke 10:19). But Jesus reminded them to emphasize their position in heaven more than their power on earth (Luke 10:20).

When you rejoice more over your heavenly standing than over your earthly status, God lifts your life to a higher level.

Because of our heavenly standing we will inherit eternal life in heaven (Luke 10:25-28). Eternal life is a quantity of life without end, and a quality of life without pain or pleasure. God wants us to sing the praises of going to heaven when we die.

Because of our heavenly standing we should show mercy on earth (Luke 10:30-37). Mercy is the special and immediate regard to eliminate the misery of another. We should show mercy to those who care nothing about us or our ancestors. The Jews cared nothing for Samaritans, yet the Samaritan in the scripture referenced above cared deeply for the needs of the Jew who had been robbed and beaten. Likewise, we should show mercy expecting nothing in return.

When you emphasize your heavenly standing over your earthly status, God lifts your life to a higher level. Therefore, emphasize what you prioritize.

EMPHASIZE

Questions

1. What did you emphasize most yesterday? Today?

2. How would God concur with your emphasis?

3. What neighborly mercy did you show yesterday? Today?

4. How will God concur with your neighborly mercy?

Observations

- Because of my standing in heaven, I have a hopeful heart.

- Because of my standing in heaven, I have a helpful hand.

Chapter 10

MAKING IT ON BROKEN PIECES

"For even though I am absent in body, nevertheless I am with you in spirit, rejoicing to see your good discipline and the stability of your faith in Christ."

—Colossians 2:5

HAVE YOU EVER FELT A SENSE OF DESPERATION? Have you ever believed that disaster had been signed, sealed, and delivered to your residence? If so, what did you do?

Because the apostle Paul preached the resurrection, the Jewish authorities brought many unsubstantiated allegations against him (Acts 25:1-2, 7). They charged him with preaching against the Law, the temple, and Caesar. None of the charges were true and when he boldly declared his innocence, they requested a trial in Jerusalem (Acts 25:8). However, the Jews never intended to have a trial, they planned to kill him on the way (Acts 25:3).

As a Roman citizen, Paul exercised his rights and appealed to Caesar; he wanted to stand trial in Rome (Acts 25:9-12). Eventually, he and two hundred seventy-five others set sail toward Rome (Acts 27:1, 6, 37).

When they approached the island of Crete, a hurricane type wind descended upon them (Acts 27:14). After many days of wavering on the waters, they surrendered to the notion of death (Acts 27:20). However, despite their lost hope God guided them safely to land (Acts 27:44).

I must tell you, that you will make it when you try. Your active faith in God will rescue you even when all human hope has vanished away.

How Can I Activate My Faith When There Is No Hope?

Consider the evidences for hope. Consider all that the Lord has said regardless of how long ago it was when He last said it. The passage of time does not negate the statements of God.

Though some time had passed since God told Paul that he would send him to the Gentiles, Paul knew that because God had said so it would be done (Acts 22:21). Paul also knew that God had said he would be a witness in Rome (Acts 23:11).

Believe all the evidences for hope. Believe all that the Lord has said regardless of how long ago it was when He last said it. Passage of time does not negate the promises of God.

Before the storm, Paul believed that he would arrive in Rome (Acts 19:21). During the storm, his belief (faith) never wavered. He continually believed that he would arrive in Rome as God had said (Acts 27:23-25).

Behave according to all the evidences for hope. Do all that the Lord has said regardless of how long ago it was when He last said it. Paul stayed in the ship (Acts 27:31-32) and he ate food in the ship as well (Acts 27:33-38).

Having no human hope is a most unpleasant situation. Nevertheless, we can recuperate even when all hope has dissipated. Observing the ways in which Paul, through faith, recuperated brings hope to us.

The ship's passengers made it to land on the broken pieces of the ship. Likewise, we will make it when we try. Our active faith in God will rescue us even when all human hope has vanished away.

Never, never, never, give up! Even when all hope has vanished away, never give up. God wants you to reaffirm your faith even when all hope is gone. How? Locate a promise of God that speaks to your situation in life. Believe it and then behave it into existence.

▲ ▲

God Himself is family. Using the plural "Us" when He verbalized His thoughts about human beings, seems to indicate the family essence of God (Genesis 1:26). God designed that family unit for after fashioning man and woman He brought them together to be family (Genesis 1:27-28). He designed the family unit to fulfill the basic human need for socialization He had created within human beings (Genesis 2:18-25). By design God created human to be family.

The family is God's oldest organism. He is the Executive Creator and He seeks to be the Executive Administrator of the family. When He is honored and adored for a His executive authority, family functions effectively.

▼ ▼

PART 2

FAMILY

Chapter 11

WHAT'S CHARACTER GOT TO DO WITH IT?

THE TEMPLE AUTHORITIES DEMANDED TO KNOW the source of Jesus' authority (Matthew 21:23). Deciding to play the intellectual game of juxtaposition, Jesus asked them a question. Using an intellectual proposal, He asked them what was the source of John's (John the Baptist) baptism (Matthew 21:24-25a). They pondered the simplicity of His question, but though the question was simple, they knew they had better tread cautiously considering the enormity of the implications of their answer. For they knew that if they admitted that John's baptism was from heaven, Jesus would ask why did they not obey it. They also knew that they could not say that John's baptism was from man, for everyone knew that John was a prophet of God. Therefore, they said that they could not tell. With a simple multiple choice question, Jesus exposed their lack of character (Matthew 21:25b-27).

> Everyone wants others to have character, but few are willing to pay the price to gain it for themselves.

Everyone wants others to have character, but few are willing to pay the price to gain it for themselves. Ever wonder why there are no character seminars? I want you to have character, but when I sign you up for the character course you refuse to attend. You want me to have character, but when you sign me up for the course I exempt myself. For some reason, character seems to be more valuable in others than in ourselves.

What Really Is Character?

Character is the willingness to do right. In the midst of the mountain of gray areas, there is still some black and white. Some "rights" and some "wrongs" still remain.

Character is the willingness to do right as God defines it. As the Law Giver, God exercises divine authority and administrative ownership over everything that exists or has ever existed (Exodus 4:10-13; Isaiah 6:1, 8, 11). He, Himself, absolutely establishes the standard of right and wrong. When consequentialism, majority rule, and intuition have exhausted their finiteness, morality positions itself upon the shoulders of God Almighty.

Not only is there a Law Giver, there is a Law given. When all has been said about grace, there is a Law given (Romans 7:22-25) that shows us what we should be. The Holy Spirit pushes us to be what we can be, while Jesus Christ shows us what we will be. We must submit to rules that we did not vote on because there is a system of right and wrong for which we had no input. Therefore, we must develop the will to do what is right as God defines right.

Character is the willingness to do right, as God defines it, because that is what we should do. Character also causes us to do right, as God defines it, for instrumental reasons. A great degree of good is done and damage prevented by doing right. Shadrach, Meshach, and Abed-nego declared that they would serve God, for they believed that God was able to deliver them (Daniel 3:15-17). They anticipated some good would result from their steadfast allegiance to their God, yet there is more.

Character causes us to do right, as God defines right, for intrinsic reasons. The human mind is often incapable of perceiving much of the good that results from our obedience to God. Obedience allows us to escape a guilty conscience, but we must commit to maintaining our character. Others before us have, as will others after us.

Shadrach, Meshach, and Abed-nego declared that they would serve God, even if He did not deliver them (Daniel 3:13-18). They would do right just because it was right to do so. God is always right and He made us in His image. Therefore, He wants us to do what is right because it reflects His nature.

However, doing right does not always produce a noticeable benefit. Sometimes we must do right just to maintain our character. Not only does the obvious benefit often escape our notice, there may occasionally be a cost of doing right. Nevertheless, character demands that we do what is right because it is right, regardless of the cost.

It is easier to maintain a peaceful relationship with people of character. They are dependable and we love dependable people because they make life more enjoyable for everyone involved. People of character are also predictable. We love predictable people for they make life more enjoyable as well.

Let us never become like the tabloid reporters who reminded Jesus of two tragedies (Luke 13:1-5):

- That Pilate had killed some Galileans and mingled their blood with the blood of their sacrifice.

- A tower in Siloam that fell killing eighteen people.

What terrible tragedies! The reporters perceived that a character flaw led to these tragedies (John 9:1-4) and believed that the character of the victims had brought this ill fate upon them.

The character of the victims was more of an issue to the reporters than their own character was to themselves, so Jesus confronted them about their character flaw. God wants us to let Him reconstruct our character; so with sincere character let's pray this prayer:

> *God always give me the conscious wisdom to know what is right and the courageous will to do what is right.*

IMPEDIMENTS TO CHARACTER DEVELOPMENT

Empty philosophies impede our march toward character development. Subscribing to the philosophy that our personal fulfillment takes precedent over our character is one example. When how good we feel becomes more important than who we are, character development takes a back seat. If, when the defining moment arrives at discipleship junction, we choose our personal fulfillment over character, we will continue a downward drift.

A new morality surfaces defined by how we feel. We begin to adopt the philosophy that whatever provides for our personal fulfillment, even if only temporary, is right and whatever stands in the way of our personal fulfillment is wrong. We will say, *"I know what the Bible says, but God wants me to be happy."* Do away with such nonsense! We must choose pain over pleasure, as Moses did, in order to be a person of character (Hebrews 11:24-27).

Subscribing to the philosophy that our professional future takes precedent over our character, impedes character development as well. When how far we advance professionally becomes more important than who we are, character gets shoved aside. If, when the defining moment arrives at discipleship junction, we choose our professional future over character, we will continue our downward drift.

With a new ethic surfaces, defined by how far we advance, we begin to adopt the philosophy that: 1) whatever promotes our professional future, even if only temporarily, is right, and, 2) whatever stands in the way of our professional future is wrong. We know what the Bible says, but God wants us to advance.

You may wonder why this much information about character is in the family section of this book. Presently, it appears that there are more forms of personal fulfillment than could have ever been imagined. Unimaginable strides have been made in our professional future, yet we have difficulty maintaining thriving, long-term marriage relationships.

Character is the oil that minimizes the friction in our relationships.

We may win at work and play, but lose in our relationships. Why? An absence of character is the culprit. Character is the oil that minimizes the friction in our relationships. When personal fulfillment or professional future takes precedent over character, relationships deteriorate. When character is no longer pursued, the friction destroys relationships. The breakdown of relationships is a hefty price to pay for temporary fulfillment and/or an empty professional future.

People who once fit together, no longer fit due to the lack of character that deteriorated their relationship. Therefore, people who once loved each other more than anyone else in the world, now hate each other more than anyone else in the world.

Character is a crucial ingredient necessary for family peace and tranquility. When character goes, we begin to think like this: *"I ought to be accepted just the way I am."* However, we do not accept our children just the way they are. Children have biological character tendencies that we discipline them away from. By nature, children are selfish cry babies, who put everything they get their hands on into their mouth. God does not accept nor allow His children to forever remain immature. He challenges us to mature and behave likewise (1 Corinthians 13:11). Therefore, we must put in place a method that develops our actions toward building character.

Abiding is a behavior that develops character. The life of the vine flows through the branches (John 15:5-7). Jesus is the vine and we are the branches. Therefore, His life flows into us when we abide in Him. The word "abiding" is a highly relational word. To abide, is to remain, stay, stay close, move in with, live with, and/or vacation with. Connected association greatly influences human thought and action. This was evident with those who experienced a connected association with Jesus (Acts 4:13). Even when His disciples denied their connected association, it was still evident (Matthew 26:73).

How Do We Abide?

Think and behave as if Christianity is a relationship first and foremost that produces our religion. Think and behave as if Christianity is about associating in such a way as to cause us to imitate those with whom we associate.

God, being in the image of Christ, grew the saints toward their ultimate conclusion (Romans 8:29). He said *"work out your own salvation"* which meant to carry to the ultimate conclusion, just as a student works out a problem in mathematics (Romans 5:3, 15:18; 2 Corinthians 7:10-11; James 1:3). God designed us to become changed from the inside out, so He is at work within us (Philippians 2:13). Therefore, we can work with God or we can work against Him. Abiding is how we work with Him.

God renews us through the taking-off of our old self (Titus 3:3-7, Ephesians 4:17-22) and through the putting-on of our new self (Titus 3:8-11, Ephesians 4:23-32). A renewed mind removes our natural resistance to the work (rule) of God in our life. Removing our natural resistance to the word and work of God gives Him greater authority over our will (character). Only when our character changes will we make sense of things that previously seemed ridiculous (i.e. forgiveness, loving our enemies, submission). As believers, we do not automatically change; God has to change us.

How Did Our Character Become Corrupted?

Through lies of deception, the adversary corrupted human character. The serpent deceived Eve and the rest is history (Genesis 3:1-13, John 8:44).

Thank God for Jesus Christ! He has made a way for us to become free. The truth that we know and can recall at the moment, has the capacity to make us free from the lies that corrupt our character (John 8:32). Continuing (abiding) in the word gives us he capacity to know the truth. This frees us from the lies that corrupt our character (John 8:31). Continuing in the word is how we take off our old lifestyle of lies and deception that corrupts our character.

How Do We Continue in the Word?

We consciously combat each specific lie with a specific truth from the word of God, in order to continue in the word (Matthew 4:1-10). Jesus maintained the integrity of His character by successfully resisting the temptation of the adversary. When Satan tempted Jesus, He did not pray, but quoted scripture instead. Pray before you enter temptation (Matthew 26:41, Mark 14:38, Luke 22:40, 46) and once you enter temptation, quote scripture (Luke 4:1-13).

Upon conversion, God changes our heart instantly but educates our mind slowly (2 Corinthians 5:17-21, Romans 12:1-2). Therefore, we will never be free until we know the truth. We will never be able to take off, so that God can fully develop our character, until we first begin to continue in the word.

Biblical imperatives, apart from spiritual thinking, lead to short term obedience and long term frustration. Beliefs shape our attitudes and actions. False beliefs shape negatively, while positive beliefs shape positively.

Consciously conforming each specific aspect of life to a specific truth from the word of God is how to continue in the word (Matthew 4:1-10). You must conform your…

- …thinking to a specific truth from the word of God, in order to create healthy thoughts within your own heart (Philippians 4:7-9)

- …speech to a specific truth from the word of God, so that you begin to utter words of life instead of death (Ephesians 4:29)

- …appearance to a specific truth from the word of God, so you may bring honor to God (1 Corinthians 11:1-16).

Haggling over God's edicts constitute rebellious contentiousness—the equivalent to witchcraft (1 Samuel 15:23). Participation in witchcraft certainly suggests a character flaw.

WHAT'S CHARACTER GOT TO DO WITH IT?

> ▶ When you hold knowledge in your mind, only then can you consciously combat each specific lie with a specific truth from the word of God.

God wants you to memorize scripture. The truth that you know and can recall at a moment's notice has the capacity to set you free from the lies that corrupt your character. When you hold knowledge in your mind, only then can you consciously combat each specific lie with a specific truth from the word of God. Likewise, when you hold knowledge in your mind, only then can you consciously conform each aspect of your life to a specific truth from the word of God.

Family is a God idea. We need not go any further, unless we are going to be people of character. Without the will to do right, conflict becomes circular. The husband says, *"I would have done ... but she did not do."* The wife says, *"I would have done ... but he did not do."* Then confusion sets in about what is the cause and what is the effect.

Therapists cannot monitor our relationships. Character integrity is our most adequate monitor. Without it, workable solutions provide no benefit. Now that you have decided to be a person of character and integrity, honestly examine what is right as God defines right.

What Has Character Got to Do With It?

Everything! Character flaws will constantly sabotage relationships so they can never improve as long as these flaws dominate. All relationship participants must covenant to do right, as God defines right, [regardless of the cost] because it is right to do right.

Chapter 12

A GOD-CENTERED IDENTITY

GOD HAS A PREFERENCE FOR WHAT HE WANTS. Yet, He also has a tolerance for what He will accept. God may even regulate what He just tolerates.

God's preference is His ideal will, while His tolerance is His circumstantial will. Living perfectly sinless is God's preference and His ideal will (1 John 2:1), but trusting in the advocacy of Jesus when we sin is His tolerance, His circumstantial will.

What God wants and what God accepts are two separate issues. Scripture certifies what God wants but what He will accept are not identical.

What God wants is His ideal will, but what God accepts is His circumstantial will. Living without sin is God's ideal will. Yet, He accepts those who sin, but who also trust in Jesus as their advocate (1 John 2:1).

God positioned Himself to be Israel's only King. Therefore, He gave judges, not kings to rule over His people, Israel (Deuteronomy 16:18). Years later, the people fired God and demanded a king so they could be like the nations surrounding them (1 Samuel 8:5). God labeled their request as a rejection of Him, a further extension of their having already forsaken Him (1 Samuel 8:7). Though their request dishonored God, He actually chose their king for them (1 Samuel 9:15-16). Imagine that, God selecting the king that He did not want them to have. In addition to selecting their king, God provided instructions and blessings for him.

Once again, this experience indicates that God may use that which He does not approve. Subsequently, God may even give instructions to regulate what He initially did not approve. What God wants and what God accepts are two separate issues. Scripture certifies what God wants, and what He will accept are not identical. What God wants is His ideal will, but what God accepts is His circumstantial will. Living without sin is God's ideal will. Yet, He accepts those who sin but trust in Jesus as their advocate (1 John 2:1).

A God-Centered Identity

God's Intended Relationship *Before* Sin Corrupted It

From the beginning, God designed human relationships. From the ideal beginning, we read about the exquisite beauty of the fellowship Adam and Eve had with their Creator. They were able to walk and talk with God and enjoy intimate fellowship with Him. Adam and Eve literally experienced having the Lord *"come walk with them in the cool of the evening"* (Genesis 3:8-9). The good news is that today we, too, can partake in this intimate relationship. God has provided us with both the information and capacity to rectify dysfunctional relationships in our lives.

Have you ever noticed that the farther we travel from inception, the farther we wander away from the original pattern? For example, when children learn to write from a model, the less adequate their writing becomes. The same is true when we reproduce recordings or copies. The more generations away from the original, the more the copy becomes degraded. Therefore, it behooves us to make each copy from the master, not from a copy of the master.

Likewise, it behooves us to juxtapose our family alongside the original design that God provided. Therein, we can see the ideal and ultimate will of God before sin marred it. As we sculpt our family using God's blueprint, it is essential to establish that there can be only one source of truth upon which to build and correct our relationships. That standard must be the holy, inerrant Word of God. When we demonstrate our willingness to submit and adjust our lives to the

Word and spurn advice stemming merely from our culture, our media (Oprah or Dr. Phil), our friends, or traditions, then and only then, will we be able to experience human relationships, as intended by God.

In the beginning, God created human beings in His own image: *"God created man in His own image, in the image of God He created him; male and female He created them"* (Genesis 1:27). What is the "image of God?" Scholars have long disagreed, but what can we definitively know? Image signifies a likeness and representation (Genesis 5:3, Numbers 33:52, 1 Samuel 6:5). The image of God was not lost when Adam sinned. Our consciousness of the image of God governs present human behavior (Genesis 9:6, James 3:9). God created both male and female in His image.

Some have advocated that the image of God represented that which was consistent with His character and His Spirit. Very likely, God placed His divine imprint within the human being and made a holy impression upon His human creation. He created humans, not to look like Him physically, as God is spirit, but He gave humankind a divine essence like Himself. Being of the spiritual identity with God, human beings possess His character and His spirit, resulting in consciousness and a conscience.

Others have advocated that the image of God is His representation to relate and rule within the universe. God endowed human beings with His authority to exercise dominion within the created order.

A GOD-CENTERED IDENTITY

Therefore, when God created the male and female in His image, He gave them a God-centered identity. This identity has to do with how we see ourselves relating to others as individuals.

To be in the image and likeness of God does not mean to possess some physical attributes of God, for *"God is spirit"* (John 4:24). A spirit does not have flesh and bones (Luke 24:39).

To be in the image and likeness of God does mean to possess the capacity to speak God's (good) words and perform God's (good) works. Jesus is the image of God (Colossians 3:15). When Philip demanded to be shown the father, Jesus honored his request by calling Philip's attention to His words and works (John 14:1-12). Those who are born again are renewed in the image and likeness of God (Ephesians 4:24, Colossians 3:10).

> Being created in the image and likeness of God means we have the capacity to speak good words and perform good works.

Being created in the image and likeness of God means we have the capacity to speak good words and perform good works. Jesus provides our best opportunity for understanding concepts of God, as it is He who explains God to us and for us, *"No one has seen God at any time; the only begotten God who is in the bosom of the Father, He has explained*

Him" (John 1:18). The word "explained" is our English word "exegesis," which literally means *to lead out*. Therefore, Jesus leads God out from behind the curtain of invisibility into full view. That is why Jesus Himself is said to be *"the image of the invisible God"* (Colossians 1:15).

Jesus will explain the image of God for us as we read about His conversation with Philip. When Philip asked Jesus to show him the Father, Jesus said to him, *"Have I been so long with you, and yet you have not come to know Me, Philip? He who has seen Me has seen the Father; how can you say, 'Show us the Father'?"* (John 14:9). Jesus then proceeded to talk about the words that He spoke and the works that He did. Jesus is the image of God, yet He wrapped His identity within His words and His works. Jesus' identity image was and is His words and His works.

Why Combine Words And Works?

From the beginning, God did His works through His words. Time and time again He said, *"Let there be",* and *"there was"* (Genesis 1:3, 6, 9, 11, 14, 20, 24, 26). Jesus did His works through His words. Jesus said to the demons that inhabited the man in the synagogue in Capernaum, *"come out of him,"* and they did (Mark 1:25). He said to the wind of the Sea of Galilee, *"be still,"* and the wind died down (Mark 4:39). God has created us in His image and has created us to behave like Him and His Son. God created us with the capacity to speak good words and perform good works through the speaking

A GOD-CENTERED IDENTITY

of good words. It is worthy of note that when the apostle Paul reminded believers of their new self, which is created in the likeness of God, he talked most about their speech (Ephesians 4:24-32, Colossians 3:8-10).

Both male and female possess a God-centered identity, which has to do with how we see ourselves as human beings relating to other human beings. Frequently, relationships revolve around a self-centered identity. Therefore, we need to understand a God-centered identity. Let's discover some realities of our God-centered Identity to help us fully understand what it is.

If humanity honored its God-centered identity, relationship problems would soon vanish. And yes, God created us for relationships. Studying both Old and New Testament scripture, we can quickly see that God has always been concerned about us having a right relationship with Him, with one another, with our spouse, with our children, and even with our enemies. If all humans related to each other in light of a God-centered identity, human dignity would be easily restored. However, without a relationship centered on our Creator, we will have neither the spiritual guidance nor the power to rectify our broken relationships. A God-centered identity restores the health of family, church, and community relationships.

Too frequently, relationships revolve on the axis of a self-centered identity. To illustrate this, consider two fathers who are next-door neighbors. They look alike on the outside and appear to have a similar lifestyle, but there is a vast difference.

One is a good husband and father because he desires to get along with his wife and children, and he wants others to respect him. The other man is a good husband and father because he wants to please God and he understands that God has given him his wife and their children as living gifts. He understands that both his wife and children deserve his love, care, and attention. This man's desire is to please God.

Relationships that have a God-centered identity understand that true love is shown not with the tongue, *but with a towel.* Having Jesus as our Lord and Teacher, we listen as He says, *"Now that I, your Lord and Teacher, have washed your feet, you also should wash one another's feet."* Jesus said, *"I came not to be served, but to serve."* Being created in His image, we know that we are never more like Jesus than when we are serving others.

To further help us understand a God-centered identity, let's look at the male-female relationship before sin corrupted it. This will reveal God's design for male-female relationship before sin turned things upside down.

A gender war exists, but how did this relationship combat begin? Conflict between the male and female abounds in all circles—political, economic, sports, and so forth. Not content to confine itself, this contention extends itself to even the Boy Scouts, Girl Scouts, little leagues, and throughout the family. This gender war has adversely affected even Christians as the people of God have surrendered to the ungodly persuasion of self-centered identity. Self-centeredness distorts God's perspective of holy wholesomeness for male/female

A God-Centered Identity

relationships. This gender conflict has become contagious and has contaminated humanity's entire way of thinking.

 By observing and learning how Satan initiated this gender conflict, we can stop the contamination process.

By observing and learning how Satan initiated this gender conflict, we can stop the contamination process. We will see how he successfully persuaded Eve to adopt a self-centered attitude that has affected our relationships with God and one another.

First, Satan came in disguise—crafty, subtle, and more cunning than the other animals—nothing caused Eve to be alarmed by his approach. He didn't announce his presence through a bullhorn saying, *"Here I come, to rob, steal, and kill."* In fact, it seems he may have even wanted to engage Eve in a little theological chat! *"Did God really say you must not eat from any tree in the garden? I mean, can we just analyze this?"*

Next, Satan attacked God by attacking His Word. *"Now I know you don't believe that He really meant you will surely die, did you? After all that He's given you in this lovely garden, do you really think you will surely die? Come on, Eve, can we think outside of the box here?"* We must guard against falling into the same trap as Eve by stating that we believe in the truth of the Holy text, but then question whether God really means it when He says, *"...fornicators, adulterers...covetous, nor drunkards...shall not inherit the kingdom of God"* (1 Corinthians 6:9b-10b).

Finally, Satan attacked God's character (note Genesis 3:5): *"For God knows that when you eat of that tree your eyes will be opened and you will be like God, knowing good and evil."* Notice how Satan attacked God's goodness. Satan in essence said: *"God is just trying to keep you on a leash. He doesn't want you to experience the good life because He knows that when you eat of that fruit you'll be just as good as He is."* Satan disguised himself and then attacked God's Word, character, and goodness. Suddenly, self-centeredness sprang alive and lured Eve into that which was evil. Ultimately, this philosophy separated both Eve and her husband from God.

Within the first chapter of Genesis, God placed both the male and female on center stage. Therein, God gave them assignments toward the created universe: *"God blessed them; and God said to them, 'Be fruitful and multiply, and fill the earth, and subdue it; and rule over the fish of the sea and over the birds of the sky and over every living thing that moves on the earth'"* (Genesis 1:28). In the beginning, they both received the assignment of populating and the earth.

God assigned both of them to rule the earth by giving them co-dominion rights. Who did He tell to subdue the earth? He told them, male and female, to subdue the earth. What did He assign them to do after subduing the earth? He told them to rule over the earth. In the beginning, God gave co-dominion

A GOD-CENTERED IDENTITY

and the responsibility to populate the earth to both male and female. They were co-rulers of the universe.

GOD CREATED THE WOMAN *FROM* THE MAN

Within the second chapter of Genesis, God stood only the male on center stage. Therein God gave him an assignment toward the created universe: to exercise headship authority.

God created the man, Adam, from the dust of the earth, *"Then the Lord God formed man of dust from the ground, and breathed into his nostrils the breath of life; and man became a living being"* (Genesis 2:7). From the dust of the earth, God created the animal kingdom, *"Out of the ground the Lord God formed every beast of the field and every bird of the sky, and brought them to the man to see what he would call them; and whatever the man called a living creature, that was its name"* (Genesis 2:19). But God created the woman, Eve, from the rib of the man, Adam:

> *So the Lord God caused a deep sleep to fall upon the man, and he slept; then He took one of his ribs and closed up the flesh at that place. The Lord God fashioned into a woman the rib which He had taken from the man, and brought her to the man. The man said, 'This is now bone of my bones, And flesh of my flesh; She shall be called Woman, Because she was taken out of Man.'*
> —GENESIS 2:21-23

Indeed God created the woman *from* the man, *"For man does not originate from woman, but woman from man"*

(1 Corinthians 11:8). God fashioned the woman, not from the dust of the earth, but from the substance of the man.

Creating Adam first gave God time to be alone with him. Likewise, God most likely put Adam to sleep so that He could spend some time alone with the woman. Therefore, remember to spend time alone with God. Before you marry, spend intimate time alone with God. Even after you marry, spend intimate time alone with God. Consider His works. (Psalm 8:3-6) Ask Him of His (God-centered) identity.

Whereas, there may be a tremendous amount of gender abuse and violation, the solution is not to throw away the fundamental, foundational principle that God has given us. Just make sure that you establish your relationship upon that biblical foundation. When you trust in the counsel of God for your relationships, you will be blessed. Consider the blessings and the consequences of it in both Psalm 1 and Jeremiah 17.

"Blessed is the man who does not walk in the counsel of the wicked nor stand in the path of sinners, nor sit in the seat of scoffers" (Psalms 1:1) versus "Cursed is the man who trusts in mankind" (Jeremiah 17:5a).

"But his delight is in the law of the Lord and in it he meditates day and night" (Psalms 1:2) As opposed to *"And makes flesh his strength and whose heart turns away from the Lord."* (Jeremiah 17:5b).

"And he will be like a tree firmly planted by streams of water which yields its fruit in its season, and its leaf does not wither, and in whatever he does he prospers" (Psalms 1:4) rather than *"For he will be like a bush is the desert and*

A God-Centered Identity

will not see when prosperity comes, but will live in stony wastes in the wilderness, a land of salt without inhabitant" (Jeremiah 17:6).

God Created The Woman *for* the Man

The Bible contains God's stated purpose for creating the woman; she was created to meet the needs of the already existing man, *"Then the Lord God said, 'It is not good for the man to be alone; I will make him a helper suitable for him'..... The Lord God fashioned into a woman the rib, which He had taken from the man, and brought her to the man. The man said, 'This is now bone of my bones, And flesh of my flesh; She shall be called Woman, Because she was taken out of Man. For this reason a man shall leave his father and his mother, and be joined to his wife; and they shall become one flesh. And the man and his wife were both naked and were not ashamed'"* (Genesis 2:18-25).

Indeed, the woman was created *for* the man, *"for indeed man was not created for the woman's sake, but woman for the man's sake"* (1 Corinthians 11:9). The woman enabled the man to lead a fulfilled life.

After God created the man, He took him to His Garden *"The Lord God planted a garden toward the east, in Eden; and there He placed the man whom He had formed"* (Genesis 2:8). Please note the sequence of events here. Adam first spent time alone with God. Then God gave Adam a residence; his address was East of Eden. God then gave Adam a job, *"to dress it and keep"* the Garden (Genesis 2:15). It was only after this that Adam was given a wife. Then God created the woman and He took her to her career, the man, *"The Lord God fashioned into a woman the rib which He had taken from the man, and brought her to the man"* (Genesis 2:22). Healthier relationships occur when our relationships with one another are God-Centered, and we are more able to recognize and encourage this in others.

Some mental health professions see a link between career and personal self-concept. The "Trait Factor Counseling Model" subscribes to the belief that when a person is constructively engaged in productive work, he will enjoy maximum psychological health. But, one could never be mentally healthy unless he was industriously engaged.

God's Intended Relationship *After* Sin Corrupted It

God referred to the woman whom He had taken off center stage. Because of sin, God executed a penalty against her and everything no longer existed solely for her comfort. He multiplied the pain of an already existing condition, *"To the woman He said, 'I will greatly multiply Your pain in childbirth, In pain you will bring forth children; Yet your desire will be for your husband, And he will rule over you'"* (Genesis 3:16).

Sin corrupted the woman's relationship toward her husband taking her backstage where the adversarial relationship developed. Now, the woman would desire and seek to possess and control her husband, *"Yet your desire will be for your husband"* (Genesis 3:16b). This word "desire" refers to the sin of wanting to possess and control. It is the same word used to describe the desire of sin to possess and control Cain, *"If you do well, will not your countenance be lifted up? And if you do not do well, sin is crouching at the door; and its desire is for you, but you must master it"* (Genesis 4:7).

God also took man off the stage as He executed his penalty against him. Because of sin, God executed a penalty against him and everything no longer existed solely for man's comfort, God multiplied the pain of an already existing condition:

> *"Then to Adam He said, 'Because you have listened to the voice of your wife, and have eaten from the tree about which I commanded you, saying, "You shall not eat from it"; Cursed is the ground because of you; In toil you will eat of it All the days of your life. Both thorns and thistles it shall grow for you; And you will eat the plants of the field; By the sweat of your face You will eat bread, Till you return to the ground, Because from it you were taken; For you are dust, And to dust you shall return."*
> —Genesis 3:17-19

Sin also corrupted the man's relationship toward his wife and took him backstage, which is where the adversarial relationship developed. Now, the man would desire to dominate his wife, *"And he will rule over you"* (Genesis 3:16c). This word "rule" means "to dominate." It is the same word translated as "master" and described the charge for Cain to rule over the sin that desired to possess and control him, *"but you must master it"* (Genesis 4:7).

So how are we to turn our relationships from self-centered to God-Centered? We must put on His nature to have His heart. Think about it, if Jesus were physically on the earth today, what do you suppose He would be doing? He would be sharing the gospel, visiting the sick, preaching to the lost, comforting, encouraging, caring, and loving people. Likewise, making our relationships God-Centered is best exemplified by our willingness to *serve as Jesus served.*

Chapter 13

WHAT IS MARRIAGE?

SADLY, WE OFTEN HEAR MORE NEGATIVE STATEments about marriage than positive. Today, many people slander the very idea of a marriage relationship. Suspicious single folk, despondent divorced folk, and maladjusted married folk regularly belittle the idea and ideal of a marriage relationship. Nevertheless, Jehovah God expects each Christian to reinforce *His* idea and ideal of marriage.

What Is God's Idea And Ideal for Marriage?

God, by means of the Holy Spirit, declared that marriage was to be honored by all. Hebrews 13:4 reads, *"Marriage is to be held in honor among all, and the marriage bed is to be undefiled; for fornicators and adulterers, God will judge".* The writer of the Hebrew letter selected the same Greek word, *timios*, that the apostle Peter used to describe the blood of Jesus and the promises of God (1 Peter 1:19 and 2 Peter 1:4). The word *'honored'* was translated from the same Greek word, *timios*, as the word *'precious'*. Therefore, we could say that marriage is as precious to God as the blood of Christ and should be honored as such.

Honorable Covenant

Marriage is a covenant (Malachi 2:10-14), a determined, ratified, and binding committed agreement. Furthermore, marriage is a covenant between a man and a woman (Genesis 2:22-24). God never permits, in fact He disallows, same sex unions that attempt to qualify as marriage (Romans 1:24-32). Some argue that same sex "partners" should have medical benefits and property rights. Medical benefits and property rights are separate issues from what constitutes marriage. We can entertain these rights without recognizing the relationship as a marriage as parents and children exercise medical benefits and property rights, yet their relationship is not referred to as a marriage.

Marriage is a bilateral covenant that obligates two persons, a man and a woman and includes both an "offer and an acceptance." In marriage the man and woman both offer themselves to the other person and accepts the other person as a spouse.

WHAT IS MARRIAGE?

The wedding vows usually express this transaction. Scripture presents the condensed version of the bilateral marriage covenant in Genesis 2:21-23, and the expanded version of the bilateral marriage covenant in Genesis 24:1-67.

Marriage is a bilateral covenant between a man and a woman witnessed by our Lord. God ordained marriage (Genesis 2:18-24) and Jesus both endorsed marriage and exalted it (Matthew 19:3-9).

Marriage is a witnessed bilateral covenant between a man and a woman for companionship (Genesis 2:18-25), that provides an environment for a husband to become one with his wife (Genesis 2:18-25). In marriage, two independent people become dependent upon their interdependency with each other. Marriage is the union and *covenant* between a man and a woman to live together as husband and wife according to the standard set by God. A covenant is a determined and ratified agreement (Malachi 2:10-14); therefore, marriage is a divine institution of God. It provides the means for intimate fellowship between husband and wife for their pleasure and for procreation—having children (Genesis 2:18-25, 1 Corinthians 7:1-5).

Marriage is for life (Matthew 19:3-8); therefore, God vehemently disapproves of dishonoring and/or breaking His covenant (Malachi 2:10-16; Romans 1:18-32; 1 Corinthians 6:9-11). Fidelity to the LORD'S covenant and its teaching is the central theme that dominates Malachi's thoughts. He charges his brethren to remain faithful to their wives from the community of covenant and thus have godly offspring. God hates divorce and demands marital fidelity.

> Commitment to the marriage covenant is the most important element that contributes to the longevity of marriage.

Commitment to the marriage covenant is the most important element that contributes to the longevity of marriage. Too often, husbands and wives just suppose that marriage will be a continuation of their present highly sexualized courtship, while at the same time meeting their need for emotional support and nurture, social interchange, friendship, partnership, belonging, and identity. They expect their mates to make them feel happy and whole. Unfulfilled expectations erode their commitment to remain married, thus commitment is the longevity key that keeps the marriage bond locked in place.

In Romans Chapter 1 verses 18-32, Paul's letter warns of God's judgment upon the people for their sins. He reminded them how their women had exchanged natural heterosexual intercourse with men for unnatural homosexual activity with women. Paul also reminded them how their men had exchanged natural heterosexual intercourse with women for unnatural homosexual activity with men. God called these deeds shameless acts and reminded them of the due penalty for their error. Make no mistake; God's wrath is against all ungodliness and unrighteousness.

God says those who continue to willingly and knowingly break His laws are worthy of death. Should not those who give their hearty approval to the selling of drugs receive the same penalty as those who sell the drugs? Does not the mafia leader who orders the "hit" receive the same penalty as the mafia members who carry out the murder?

> *Or do you not know that the unrighteous will not inherit the kingdom of God? Do not be deceived; neither fornicators, nor idolaters, nor adulterers, nor effeminate, nor homosexuals, nor thieves, nor the covetous, nor drunkards, nor revilers, nor swindlers, will inherit the kingdom of God?*
> —1 CORINTHIANS 6:9-10

Now that we have established God's viewpoint regarding the seriousness and consequences of breaking His covenants, let's discover His other requirements for marriage.

God ordained (sanctioned, legalized) the first marriage (Adam and Eve), *"God blessed them; and God said to them Be fruitful and multiply. . ."* (Genesis 1:28). This blessing given by the highest legal Authority, Jehovah God Himself, can be compared to a minister, pastor, judge or any person licensed to marry, saying, *"I now pronounce you husband and wife. You may now kiss the bride."*

When we heed God's instructions, which include obeying secular laws, the name of each party to the union is kept above reproach. Any children born into the union are spared the shame that falls on those whose parents are not married. Furthermore, a legal marriage between a man and a woman, safeguards the property rights of family members in the event of death of either spouse.

Jehovah God expects each Christian to reinforce *His* idea of marriage. We must therefore, speak honorably of the idea of marriage. Even when your marriage is below your anticipated comfort level, still speak honorably. Nothing is wrong with the institution of marriage. The problems lie not with the principle of marriage, but with the two persons in the marriage. There was nothing wrong with the Garden of Eden. The problem surfaced in Adam and Eve, the two people God placed there.

Chapter 14

GOD RECOMMENDED HONORABLE COVENANT—FOR YOUR BENEFIT

MARRIAGE IS FOR ADULTS WHO CAN LEAVE father and mother and bond emotionally with a spouse. To become married, an individual must be willing to share innermost thoughts and feelings with a spouse. Anyone who is so attached to parents or another person that he or she cannot relinquish that bond and responsibly bond with a spouse is unprepared for marriage.

Yes, marriage is only for adults who have achieved mature spiritual, moral and emotional stability.

Who Are the Mature?

Jesus developed into a fully mature individual, *"And Jesus kept increasing in wisdom and stature, and in favor with God and men"* (Luke 2:52). Full maturity should be the goal of every person.

What Constitutes Full Maturity?

Growing physically is a part of full maturity. Jesus increased in stature; growing physically is both natural and normal. You may have notched your growth and compared it to your siblings, because physical growth satisfies self-esteem needs.

Growing intellectually is a part of full maturity. Jesus increased in wisdom. When His parents returned to look for Him, Jesus was discussing weighty issues with the learned men of the day (Luke 2:46-47). Therefore, we should exercise our intellectual faculties, expand our intellectual capacity and amaze others with our wisdom.

Growing spiritually is a part of full maturity. Jesus increased in favor with God, recognizing the priority of His father's affairs, *"And He said to them, 'Why is it that you were looking for Me? Did you not know that I had to be in My Father's house?'"* (Luke 2:49). Constantly ensure your personal and corporate spiritual growth.

Growing socially is a part of full maturity. Jesus increased in favor with other human begins, engaging in dialogue with people. Be personable. Ask appropriate questions (open ended and open door) and invite people to discover for themselves.

Who Are the Mature?

The mature are those who have developed the following attributes:

- The capacity to be reliable
- An ability and willingness to give more on any job than is asked for
- The persistence to carry out plans despite the difficulty
- The ability to work with others within an organization and under authority
- The ability to make decisions
- A will to live
- The flexibility, independence and tolerance needed to succeed

On a scale from one to ten, rate yourself and your prospective mate. After both have rated each other, share and compare your ratings.

Retrospectively reflecting upon His creation, God saw that it was good. Six times He stated that it was good (Genesis 1:4; 10; 12; 18; 21; 25; 31); but, when He saw the aloneness of

Adam he said that it was not good (Genesis 2:18). Did God speak correctly when He said that it was not good for man to be alone? Whatever God says is good is good, but what God says is not good is certainly not good.

Why Was Adam's Aloneness Not Good?

God instilled within Adam an inherent need to relate to other human beings. Although he had the animal kingdom and the plant kingdom, neither of them could satisfy Adam's aloneness. Adam needed a wife, and God wanted him to have one.

You have the same needs as Adam (Matthew 19:10; 1 Corinthians 7:9). Through marriage you can satisfy your human relationship needs better than you can through anything else.

Adam experienced the perfect challenge for his body. He enjoyed abundant physical resources (Genesis 2:7-14, 16). However, despite the abundance of physical resources, he was still in a state of "not good" aloneness. The marriage relationship provided something that he needed that physical resources could never provide.

Adam experienced the perfect challenge for his mind. He enjoyed awesome intellectual responsibilities (Genesis 2:5; 15; 17; 19-20). However, despite Adam's intellectual responsibilities he was still in a state of "not good" aloneness. The marriage relationship provided something that he needed that intellectual responsibilities could never provide.

Adam experienced the perfect challenge for his soul. He enjoyed articulate spiritual relationship (Genesis 2:16; 19-20; 3:8-9). Nevertheless, he was still in a state of "not good" aloneness. The marriage relationship provided something he needed that spiritual relationship never could provide.

You have the same needs as Adam. Therefore, God recommends marriage for you.

Through the marriage relationship, God manages His creation (Genesis 1:26-28). God wants both male and female perspectives to exercise managerial oversight of His creation. A husband and wife who are committed and comfortable with each other will usually rule better.

Through the marriage relationship, God seeks to multiply His heritage (Genesis 1:26-27; Psalms 127:3; 1 Timothy 5:14). A mother and father who were first husband and wife provide the best environment for nurturing and developing children.

Through the marriage relationship God seeks to model His relationship for His people (Ephesians 5:31-32). Many ills surface because the female perspective is left out of management. Why else would God require an elder of the church to have a faithful wife (1 Timothy 3:2)?

 Through marriage you can satisfy your human relationship needs better than through anything else.

Through marriage, you can satisfy your human relationship needs better than through anything else. Satan would have you to believe the lie that:

- Physical resources will satisfy your human social relationship needs.

- Intellectual responsibilities will satisfy your human social relationship needs.

- Spiritual relationship will satisfy your human social relationship needs.

Some people have erroneously concluded that when they are mature and build their faith, God is all they need. This is not true. God chooses to involve other human beings in meeting a person's social needs (1 Corinthians 7:5).

If you are unmarried, please do not be pained by your marital status. You are valuable, can contribute to the kingdom, and can be saved just as readily as the married. However, please refrain from saying that you do not want a spouse when deep inside you know that you really need and want a husband/wife. Remember, what you say is what you get. But, if you choose to remain unmarried, you simply choose to not satisfy your needs in the most fulfilling way provided by God. It is okay to desire a spouse and it is alright to admit that you desire a spouse.

Chapter 15

Looking in the Wrong Places and Finding the Right Person

God spotlighted seven nations in that had enveloped themselves in gross idolatry (Deuteronomy 7:1-5; 20:18). These included:

- Hittites
- Girgashites
- Amorites

- Canaanites
- Perizzites
- Hivites
- Jebusites

God wanted His people to avoid their contaminating influence, so He prohibited them from marrying these idolatrous people (Deuteronomy 7:3; 1 Kings 11:1-2).

Many people have searched in vain for a spiritually-minded mate. Some people have compromised by marrying an unspiritual mate, while others have given up their search altogether and have become resigned to remaining unmarried.

Some people who desire a spouse often look for one in all the wrong places. Sometimes they find the right person, but usually they discover that most of the people they connect with are not spiritually-minded.

How Can You Find a Spiritually Minded Mate?

Who would have thought that Saul of Tarsus would have become an aggressive disciple of Jesus Christ (Acts 7:58; 9:1-2; 15)? God did because He saw his developable potential (Acts 9:15). Likewise, you may have to look among sinners to find a person who has developable potential. Don't give up. Keep looking for your diamond in the rough, but don't settle for one that is not of gem quality.

What are the indicators of developable potential? One indicator of developable potential is a willingness to communicate what is on the heart. Adam communicated what was on his heart (Genesis 2:22-23).

A willingness to commit to what is on the heart is also an indicator of developable potential. Adam committed to what was on his heart (Genesis 2:24; 2 Kings 5:27).

Who would have thought that Saul of Tarsus would become spiritually minded enough to give up his liberties for the good of another person (1 Corinthians 8:13)? God led him to become spiritually-minded. Therefore, before you become emotionally and socially dependent, lead your potential spouse to develop his/her potential.

What Do I Do When I Find My Diamond in the Rough?

When you discover your diamond in the rough, polish that diamond until its brilliance shines through.

How Do I Develop the Potential in a Potential Mate?

Help him/her develop spiritual communication. True communication comes from the heart (Luke 6:45), so create a spiritual environment to deposit spiritual ideas into his/her heart. Help him/her develop spiritual commitments to appreciate spiritual values (Romans 12:1-3).

I've listed below some risks so you might avoid them:

- Becoming attached and unable to break free of attachment is a risk. Therefore, before you become emotionally bonded make sure he/she has sufficiently developed. This is difficult, but is possible when you are spiritually focused (1 Timothy 5:1-2). You must decide how much progress and how much time you will invest before you decide that this is not going to work.

- Being led astray from the purity of your discipleship virtues is a risk. Before you venture forth, strengthen yourself (Deuteronomy 7:1-5). A dedicated disciple is stronger than one who is not a disciple.

Many, especially men, are looking to be rescued from an immoral environment and are looking for an alternate, (alternate from their present ungodliness) lifestyle. Real men are manufactured by the Holy Spirit.

Very often, strife within marriage grows from struggles during courtship. Therefore, pay attention to the issues and struggles you face while courting. Understand that these will not magically disappear after you say "I do" but will probably resurface with a vengeance.

God wants you to spiritually enhance the life of your potential spouse. He wants you to look and lead even if not for a mate (Luke 19:10).

Chapter 16

WHAT SHALL I BRING TO MY WEDDING?

GOD SAID MORE ABOUT MARRIAGE THAN HE SAID about the wedding. We, on the other hand, tend to say more about the wedding (the ceremony, the frills, the *trappings*) than about the marriage. Consequently, many have become more familiar with the wedding than they have with marriage.

People often come to their wedding empty. All too often, prospective wives spend endless hours planning and discussing their wedding while devoting very little, if any time, planning and discussing their marriage. Because of this disparity, many husbands and wives come to their wedding inadequately prepared (empty) for their marriage.

You should bring to your wedding a consciousness of biblical facts that will influence your marriage, including:

- God created marriage. He knows best and has provided instructions contained in the Scriptures. Obedience to these biblical principles will positively enhance your marriage relationship. Without obedience to God, your marriage will never become as fulfilling as God intends.

- God created marriage to provide companionship. Unfortunately, some have married because they were lonely and then divorced for the same reason.

- God created marriage to provide **psychological** companionship. "Then the LORD God said, 'It is not good for the man to be alone; I will make him a helper'" (Genesis 2:18). Therefore, the wife should learn how to be a complement (harmonize and add to) to her husband; the husband needs to understand his wife, according to accurate knowledge. *"You husbands, continue living with your wife, according to knowledge, assigning them honor as to the weaker vessel, (the feminine one),*

WHAT SHALL I BRING TO MY WEDDING?

> *since you are also heirs with them of the undeserved grace (favor) of life, in order for your prayers not to be hindered"* (1 Peter 3:7).

- God created marriage to provide ***physiological*** companionship (1 Corinthians 7:1-5). *"But because of immoralities, each man is to have his own wife, and each woman is to have her own husband. The husband must fulfill his duty to wife, and likewise also the wife to her husband"* (verses 2-3). *"The wife does not have authority over her own body, but the husband does; and likewise also the husband does not have authority over his own body, but the wife does.* {Wives, once you become married, you are a unit, one, so stop telling your husbands 'this is my body . . .'} *Stop depriving one another, except by agreement for a time, so that you may devote yourselves to prayer, and come together again so that satan will not tempt you because of your lack of self-control"* (verses 4-5).

You should bring to your wedding a consciousness (knowledge) of the persons who will influence your marriage.

Your spouse will influence your marriage so you need to know your prospective mate very well, including his/her spiritual condition. You need to know not just if he or she is a member of the church, but does this person really appreciate spiritual ideals and ideas. Will they nurture your spiritual progression? Will you 'complement' one another? Do you **know** what your prospective mate does after church service? How do they interact with other people? What are their outside interests?

It helps to know his or her *psychological* condition. You need to know not just how well he or she scores on an IQ exam, but also how she or he reasons and responds during stress.

It helps to know his or her *physiological* condition. No, I'm not talking about what you can see (the outer body, your perception of what is pleasing to your carnal senses). I am talking about what you can't see, the things you do not ask about, until you *see* the physical manifestations of its destruction. You need to know if he or she has an illness such as AIDS, sickle cell, leukemia or other illness that will stress the marriage relationship.

Your spouse's family will influence your marriage. You should bring to your wedding a consciousness of their existence along with some basic knowledge about who they are. You may think, *"I am not marrying them."* While this is true, you **are** marrying whom they produced. Knowing the producer helps you understand the product.

It helps to know the spiritual, psychological, and physiological health of your prospective mate's family. Has the family nurtured him or her in a healthy spiritual and psychological environment? If abuses were prevalent, how well has your spouse-to-be healed? What hereditary illnesses are prevalent and likely surface later in the marriage? Right now, it may seem like *"he is unlike his family"* or *"she is not like them."*

WHAT SHALL I BRING TO MY WEDDING?

The family model he or she now rejects, he or she may later accept—according to the magnitude of the stimulus. Many people have grown up and determined to not be like their parents, but given the same circumstances, they fall victim to the only model they have learned. Workaholic fathers and worryholic mothers often produce the same kind of children.

I am not saying that no one or even a majority never progress beyond their upbringing. I am just saying that family exposure is a factor. I am not suggesting that you should refuse to marry because deficiencies exist. What I am saying is to be aware that these liabilities may strain your marriage relationship.

The unwillingness and/or the inability to be reliable and give more on any job than is asked for, may wreck the marriage. Lack of persistence to carry out plans, despite the difficulty and/or the absence of a willingness to work well with others [in an organization and under authority] may produce problems. Those who are unable or unwilling to make decisions are pains waiting to happen. A family heritage that refuses to provide the flexibility, independence and/or tolerance needed to succeed will very likely plague your marriage.

> The wedding differs greatly from the marriage. The success of the wedding depends upon the management of rice, rings, and rituals. The success of the marriage depends upon the management of facts, folks, and frustrations.

The wedding differs greatly from the marriage. The success of the wedding depends upon the management of rice, rings, and rituals. The success of the marriage depends upon the management of facts, folks, and frustrations.

Whether you are now married or are contemplating marriage, you can improve its success by:

- Studying God's Word together regularly and praying to God for help in resolving problems (2 Timothy 3:16, 17; Proverbs 3:5, 6; Philippians 4: 6, 7)

- Applying biblical counsel and principles whether you feel that the other one is doing everything he or she should or should not (Romans 14:12; 1 Peter 3:1, 2)

- Confining sexual interest to one's own mate (Proverbs 5:15-21; Hebrews 13:4)

- Loving concern for the needs of your spouse can help safeguard against that one being tempted to wrongdoing (1 Corinthians 7:2-5).

WHAT SHALL I BRING TO MY WEDDING?

Relative Scriptures

These scriptures present God's foundation for marriage. Before entering into a marriage covenant *read* and *discuss* each of these scriptures with your prospective spouse.

- Genesis 1:26-31
- Genesis 2:18-25
- Genesis 3:16
- 1 Corinthians 7:1-5
- 1 Corinthians 11:1-3
- Ephesians 5:15-6:4
- Colossians 3:18-21
- 1 Timothy 5:7-16
- Titus 2:1-8
- 1 Peter 2:21-3:7

Chapter 17

CONFLICT RESOLUTION WITHIN THE MARRIAGE RELATIONSHIP

CONFLICT EXISTS WITHIN EVERY MARITAL RELAtionship. The question is not *if* conflict will occur but, **when** conflict will occur. Conflict occurs when a person must choose between two compelling and/or repelling demands. Nevertheless, marital relationships can exist with a minimal (manageable) amount of conflict. Awareness of the phases of conflict will help to regulate and manage it.

The first phase of conflict is the nuisance phase, the intense "discussing phase." At this phase, you feel that your

CONFLICT RESOLUTION WITHIN THE MARRIAGE RELATIONSHIP

spouse occasionally interferes with your ultimate happiness. However, both of you continue to tolerate each other physically and emotionally. During this phase, you neither intentionally retaliate physically nor emotionally. In other words, you wish your spouse would…but when your spouse does not, you remain physically and emotionally connected.

The second phase of conflict within the marital relationship is the hindrance phase, the intense "fussing phase." This is when you feel as if your spouse frequently interferes with your ultimate happiness. You continue to physically tolerate each other, but one, or maybe both of you, refuse to emotionally tolerate the other. You suppress physical retaliation to a minimum, but allow emotional retaliation to escalate. In other words, you wish your spouse would…and when your spouse does not, you remain physically connected, but emotionally you disconnect.

Did you notice that emotional conflict preceded physical conflict? Emotional conflict may be more devastating than physical conflict.

The third stage of conflict is the threat phase. I call this the "cussing phase." You have left the "discussing" phase and gone beyond the "fussing" phase. At this phase, you feel as if your spouse always interferes with your ultimate happiness. Retaliation increases. You neither physically nor emotionally tolerate your spouse. In other words, you wish your spouse would…but when your spouse does not, you withdraw both physically and emotionally.

Awareness of the full spectrum of conflict will help you to manage it. What level of conflict are you experiencing within your marital relationship?

It is important to note that the stages of conflict may change from one issue to another. Likewise, conflict levels may also change from one moment to the next.

Couples can reduce their marital conflict, but why does so much conflict exist? Many couples married even though they were ill prepared. Likely, they had received incorrect and insufficient information from parents and peers, which often ignites the fuse of marital conflict. Couples need information that is clear, specific, and practical.

Now that incorrect and insufficient information have victimized me, how do I learn to manage marital conflict?

You can learn adequate behavior from adequate models:

- Find one Christian couple who shares polite conversation with each other and model after them. Listen to how they talk to each other.

- Find one Christian couple who shares personal chemistry with each other and model after them. Look for spouses who bring a "sparkle" to the eye of each other just by their presence.

- Find one Christian couple who shares problem-solving conscience and model after them. Discover their strategies.

Conflict Resolution Within the Marriage Relationship

Conflict within the marital relationship is inevitable so you need to commit yourself to learn how to solve conflict-producing problems.

Questions

- At what stage of conflict is your relationship?

- Describe an occasion when your relationship was at the threat phase. How did you reduce the intensity of the conflict?

- Explain how the principles of Ephesians 4:26 can help reduce conflict in the marriage relationship.

Chapter 18

SINGLE PARENTING

GOD DEFINITIVELY DESIGNED THE FAMILY DYNAmic. He intended for the husband and wife team to perform the primary parenting of their children (1 Timothy 5:14-15; Ephesians 6:4).

> ▶ God knows what is best for the family so He gave us the best design.

God knows what is best for the family so He gave us the best design. This section is not designed for those who are already single parents, but for those whom we may be able

SINGLE PARENTING

to prevent from becoming single parents. I commend those who are single parenting, but that is often inconsistent with God's dynamic design. Single parenting unfairly deprives the family.

Single parenting often deprives the maternal grandparents. Usually, the mother assumes the majority of the parenting responsibility and her parents have to assist. It is unfair to saddle the grandparents with the responsibility of parenting grandchildren. Grandchildren are made to love, not to parent (just kidding). True grandparent-love helps parent the grandchildren.

Nevertheless, we must abandon the notion that we can have children and mommy and daddy will help raise them. Grandparents can supplement, but parenting children is the parents' responsibility. Even those who are married need to know that grandparents are there to supplement only as much as they are willing to offer. Grandparents are not there to supplement as much as the parents are willing to ask. Often, single parenting places physical, mental, economic, emotional, and spiritual demands upon these grandparents.

Single parenting often deprives the paternal grandparents. All too often, the father assumes little of the parenting responsibility so his parents are often estranged and isolated from the life of their grandchildren. It is unfair to create a situation wherein grandparents are alienated from their grandchildren.

Single parenting deprives the children of the experience of observing the affectionate, heterosexual bonding and modeling of their mother and father that God intended (Ephesians 5:22-33). They only spend divided time with parents, rarely, if ever, with both parents together. They are deprived of the synergy of nurture, for one plus one is more than two.

Single parenting deprives the single parent of the assistance of the other parent. God never intended for you to raise children alone outside the two parent model. Therefore, He required the uniting as husband and wife before the uniting of bodily fluids (sperm and egg). Even artificial insemination of the unmarried is inconsistent with His model. God requires marriage, not money for the raising of children. Celibacy until marriage is God's choice. Yet, He does forgive. It is not being pregnant while unmarried that is wrong, it is the getting pregnant while unmarried that is wrong (1 Corinthians 7:1-2). Nevertheless, those who repent must be treated with dignity. Just remember that God's order is: marriage, bearing children, and then guiding the house (1 Timothy 5:14).

God wants you to subscribe to and advocate in every case marriage before parenting. He wants you to subscribe to and advocate marriage all during the parenting. Anything less is God's tolerance not His preference.

Divorce costs the community. It deprives the community of the example of an enduring marital commitment. Also, divorce destroys the notion of permanence in marriage and fuels the false notion that everyone is divorcing. Divorce divides the social circle. Frequently, the divorced couple refuses to allow close friends to remain friends with both. Being a friend to one former spouse alienates from the other.

Divorce costs the children economically. Frequently, children become the custody of the mother. One survey showed that mothers suffered a 71% decrease in spendable income while the fathers enjoyed a 43% increase in spendable income.

Divorce costs the children emotionally. Every child progresses better within a healthy two-parent emotional environment. The divorce of their parents provides emotional baggage that haunts the children even in their own marriage relationships.

Divorce depresses the children's ego. They lose status as they become step-brothers and step-sisters. Their vulnerability towards abuse and incest increases.

Divorce costs the couple emotionally. There is really no such thing as divorce in the absolute sense of the term. Marriage involves a reciprocal and irrevocable investment of lives. That relationship may be altered but can never cease to exist. You may divide the property but can never go back to being single. Often, couples are alarmed at the intensity of their relationship.

Divorce costs energetically. Even after divorcing, both parents still have full parental responsibility to raise their children. The energy needed to raise children after divorcing, if invested during the marriage, may have managed the conflict and kept the marriage intact.

If we believe that God knows best, then we must admit that God's ideal of a two-parent family provides positives that unmarried parents simply cannot provide. Or, we must admit that God gave us an inferior family system.

But someone will say, *"You do not understand the intensity of my pain in this marriage."* Surveys show that only 10% of the time do both divorced former spouses say they find fulfillment after divorcing. Divorce then has a 90% failure rate—twice the failure rate for marriage.

Problems experienced by those who divorce are not greater than the problems experienced by those who remain married. Those who divorce renege on their commitment while those who remain married do not.

Usually, divorce is too expensive. Before you divorce, calculate all the costs. The known costs plus the unknown costs may just be more than you can afford to pay.

Chapter 19

STEP-PARENTING

A STEP-FAMILY OR BLENDED FAMILY IS A HOUSEhold unit where a step-parent or step-parents, a step-child or step-children live or visit regularly. A step-parent is a person who has married a spouse who has one or more children from a previous relationship and is not the real, natural or biological parent. Therefore, a step-parent is unreal, unnatural and unbiological. A step-parent could also be defined as an instant parent.

Step-children are children whose parent or parents have remarried. The step-parent's spouse may be the victim of a divorce, death or unmarried parenthood.

Biological parents have more time to adjust to parenthood as their children grow up from babyhood. Step-parents are catapulted into parenthood to suddenly manage in the role of a parent. Biological parenthood is complex but step-parenting is much more complex.

Physical adjustments must be made when one assumes the role of step-parent. Often, children are snatched out of the environment to which they have become attached and placed into a foreign environment for which they have been ill prepared.

Psychological adjustments must be made. Children are often ill prepared to change their socializing relationships and immediately begin to bond with foreign personalities. These adjustments often brew resentment, which may overflow and contaminate the husband-wife relationship.

Answering these questions may help us to see how stressful step-parenting can become.

- Should I ask my child's permission to marry?
- Should I invite the children to the wedding?
- Where should we live?
- What should my step children call me?
- Should I adopt my step children?
- How much interaction should I have with the biological parent?

In 2005, I penned my book "Show Me The Money"—7 exercises that build economic strength. The same drifts that demanded such a book are ever pressing against us in 2008. As I pondered the first chapter of that book, "How did we get in this mess," it dawned on me that our pursuit of hedonistic pleasure fuels the fires that burn away our financial wellbeing. Until we right-size toward a more altruistic society, our financial woes will continually rampage. Since I doubt that we will ever become a predominantly philanthropic nation, the need for this and other writings shall prevail.

PART 3

FINANCES

Chapter 20

GOD'S HONORARIUM— THE PORTION: ADAM

THE BIBLE BEGINS WITH THE BOLD DECLARATION that in the beginning Jehovah God created the universe (Genesis 1:1). By virtue of creation, God established Himself as the sovereign owner of the universe. Through His Holy Spirit, God revealed that the earth and all it contains belongs to Him, *"FOR THE EARTH IS THE LORD'S, AND ALL IT CONTAINS"* (1 Corinthians 10:26).

As sovereign owner, He was and is supreme and unaccountable to anyone else and all else is accountable to Him. Not only are we held accountable by God for our possessions, but we are also held accountable by our Federal, State, and Local governments.

God exercised His sovereign ownership authority rights by placing limitations upon the human beings whom He had created. He limited their diet to the above-ground plants that yielded seed and the fruit of trees that yielded seed, *"Then God said, "Behold, I have given you every plant yielding seed that is on the surface of all the earth, and every tree which has fruit yielding seed; it shall be food for you"* (Genesis 1:29). God also placed totally off limits the fruit of *"the tree of the knowledge of good and evil"* and He strictly forbade Adam to eat of this tree:

> *The LORD God commanded the man, saying, "From any tree of the garden you may eat freely; but from the tree of the knowledge of good and evil you shall not eat, for in the day that you eat from it you will surely die."*
> —Genesis 2:16-17

However, Adam rebelled against the sovereign authority of God and ate of the fruit that God told him not to eat, *"When the woman saw that the tree was good for food, and that it was a delight to the eyes, and that the tree was desirable to make one wise, she took from its fruit and ate; and she gave also to her husband with her, and he ate"* (Genesis 3:6).

God honored Adam with a gigantic job assignment by giving him the responsibility of managing the host of creation. He commanded Adam to rule the fish, birds, cattle and all creeping things (Genesis 1:26) and then He placed Adam in

GOD'S HONORARIUM—THE PORTION: ADAM

the Garden of Eden to cultivate it (Genesis 2:5-15). Both the tree of life and the tree of the knowledge of good and evil were in the garden. Therefore, Adam cultivated the ground from which both the tree of life and the tree of the knowledge of good and evil grew.

God gave to Adam the fruit of the tree of life, but retained for Himself the fruit of the tree of the knowledge of good and evil. For Adam's pay, God gave him a portion of what he produced from the earth (Genesis 1:29, 2:9, 16) and withheld for Himself a portion of what Adam produced. God commanded as an honorarium for Himself a portion of Adam's increase (Genesis 2:17). However, Adam refused to allow God to have His own honorarium and ate what God had designated for Himself.

Because Adam and Eve failed to give Him His honorarium, God multiplied the pain of childbirth for the woman, *"To the woman He said, 'I will greatly multiply Your pain in childbirth, In pain you will bring forth children...'"* (Genesis 3:16). God reminded us of the pain of childbirth in Isaiah 13:8 and 26:17, and again in John 16:21 and 1 Thessalonians 5:3.

Because Adam and Eve failed to Give Him His honorarium, God multiplied the pain of cultivating the soil for the man. God cursed—placed under a divine sentence of punishment—the ground and sent forth thorns and thistles from it (Genesis 3:17). God reminded us of the pain of cultivating the cursed earth in Genesis 4:11 and 5:29, and again in Romans 8:20-23 and Hebrews 6:7-8.

We must give God His honorarium, for failing to do so will stop the flow of blessings from God.

We must give God His honorarium, for failing to do so will stop the flow of blessings from God. When we refuse to give God Him His honorarium, God gives us pain that otherwise we would not have experienced.

God would have given Adam and Eve the pleasure of perpetually knowing only good because He had placed His "good" stamp of approval upon all of creation (Genesis 1:10, 12, 25). Before eating the forbidden fruit, they knew good (Genesis 1:10, 12, 18, 25). But after eating the forbidden fruit they came to know evil as well: *"Then the Lord God said, 'Behold, the man has become like one of Us, knowing good and evil; and now, he might stretch out his hand, and take also from the tree of life, and eat, and live forever'"* (Genesis 3:22).

God would have given them the pleasure of a perpetually renewed body for life (Genesis 2:9, 3:22-24, Revelation 2:7, 22:1-2, 14). Apparently, the power to restore health lies within the green vegetation.

We should give God His honorarium, because failing to do so stops the flow of blessings from God. When we refuse to give Him His honorarium, God withholds pleasure that otherwise He would have given to us.

GOD'S HONORARIUM—THE PORTION: ADAM

OBSERVATIONS FOR CONSIDERATION

When you refuse to give God His honorarium, you, like Eve, replace what God has said with what you have seen or think you have seen. God had said that eating the forbidden fruit would destroy their quality of life (Genesis 2:17). Eve saw that the fruit was good and thought that eating it would improve her quality of life (Genesis 3:6). What a deception!

When you cooperate with those who refuse to give God His honorarium, you replace what God has said with what they thought they had seen. God had said that eating would destroy their quality of life (Genesis 2:17). Nevertheless, Adam went along with what Eve thought she had seen, that eating the fruit would improve her quality of life (Genesis 3:6).

When you replace what God has said with what you have seen (think you have seen), or with what others have seen (think they have seen), you multiply the pain of your problems and reduce the pleasure within your life.

With Adam, God established His sovereign authority to determine the amount of His honorarium.

Chapter 21

GOD'S HONORARIUM—THE PRIORITY: ABEL

ADAM AND EVE GAVE BIRTH TO TWO SONS, CAIN and Abel. God inherently connected the Adam and Eve story of Genesis chapter two and three to the Cain and Abel story of Genesis chapter four because both stories addressed the honorarium for God.

God designated some fruit for Himself (Genesis 2:16-17). By refusing to give God His honorarium, Adam and Eve ate the fruit that God had reserved for Himself and replaced what God had said with what Eve thought she had seen (Genesis

GOD'S HONORARIUM—THE PRIORITY: ABEL

3:6). God had established the principle of receiving His honorarium first (Genesis 2:15-16).

Cain gave an honorarium to the Lord but he took his time in doing so. The Bible referred to his priority as the *"course of time"* (Genesis 4:3). Cain just brought an offering to God when he got-around-to-it. Cain's brother, Abel, also gave an honorarium to the Lord by bringing a sizeable portion from among the first-fruits of his stock (Genesis 4:4).

God often responds favorably toward our offering as He did toward the offering Abel brought before Him: *"Abel, on his part also brought of the firstlings of his flock and of their fat portions. And the Lord had regard for Abel and for his offering"* (Genesis 4:4). "Regard" means "respect" and comes from the Hebrew root word meaning "to gaze or to set one's face favorably toward."

 For the Lord to turn His face toward us is to keep in place His loving-kindness and His glory.

The apostle Peter presented the concept when he described the favor of God as His face being toward those whom He favored, *"FOR THE EYES OF THE LORD ARE TOWARD THE RIGHTEOUS, AND HIS EARS ATTEND TO THEIR PRAYER, BUT THE FACE OF THE LORD IS AGAINST THOSE WHO DO EVIL"* (1 Peter 3:12). When the Lord's face shines, He is gracious toward you. To the Israelites, Moses equated the blessings of God with Him making His face to shine upon them (Numbers 6:22-27). David prayed for the Lord to keep His face toward him so His loving-kindness would remain (2 Chronicles 6:42-7:1, 11-15). For the Lord to turn His face toward us is to keep in place His loving-kindness and His glory.

At other times, God responds unfavorably toward our offering as He did toward Cain's, *"but for Cain and for his offering He had no regard. So Cain became very angry and his countenance fell."* (Genesis 4:5). "No regard" means "disrespect." God disrespected Cain and his offering as Cain had disrespected God by bringing it. The word for no regard comes from the Hebrew root word meaning "to gaze or to set one's face unfavorably away from." For the Lord to turn His face away is to remove His loving-kindness and His glory. When God set His face against the Israelites, they became physically ill and vulnerable to their enemies (Leviticus 26:14-17, Deuteronomy 31:16-18).

God responded differently to both Abel and Cain's offering. Likewise, God may respond differently to our offering, because He responds according to the person that we are.

God responded favorably toward Abel because Abel was righteous and offered the firstlings of his flocks, which ultimately proved to be an acceptable sacrifice. His better sacrifice argues that Abel was righteous, and his righteous first-fruit sacrifice still speaks to us (Hebrews 11:4) as God responds according to the presentation that we bring. God responded favorably toward Abel because of his offering, the firstlings and the fat from his flocks (Genesis 4:4).

From Adam and Eve, God deducted His offering first (Genesis 2:15-17) and continued to require the first for His offering (Deuteronomy 12:6).

God responded unfavorably towards Cain because he was unrighteous and delayed bringing his offering. He just presented it "when he got around to it," thus His offering proved to be less acceptable than the one offered by Abel. His lesser-quality sacrifice argues that he was unrighteous. His unrighteous, when-I-get- around-to-it, attitude speaks as a warning to us (1 John 3:12). God responded unfavorably towards Cain because he did not offer the first of his fruits (Genesis 4:3). God rejects untimely gifts (Exodus 22:29, 23:19a).

Observations for Consideration

God may accept your offering and when He does so, He **blesses** you. God may reject your offering and when He does so, He **curses** you. You either live under the blessings of God or under the curse of God. He stakes His claim on your first-fruits, as the giving of your first-fruits is compatible with your spiritual nature (James 1:18). Refusing to give of your first-fruits is incompatible with your spiritual nature.

With Abel, God established His sovereign authority to receive His honorarium first.

Chapter 22

GOD'S HONORARIUM— THE PERMANENCE: ABRAHAM

JESUS CHRIST IS OUR HIGH PRIEST FOREVER (Hebrews 6:20, 7:17, 24, 28), thus the order of the priesthood to which Melchizedek belonged continues (Hebrews 7:8). Jesus Christ is high priest by the sovereign decree of God, not by genealogical heritage (Hebrews 5:10, 7:13-17, 20-22). Likewise, Melchizedek became high priest by sovereign decree of God, not by genealogical heritage (Hebrews 7:3). Jesus Christ is king of peace and righteousness (Ephesians 2:14, 1 John 2:29, 2 Peter 1:1). Likewise, Melchizedek was king of peace and righteousness (Hebrews 7:2).

GOD'S HONORARIUM—THE PERMANENCE: ABRAHAM

Earlier scripture, the Old Testament, provides historical insights into the covenant that God made with Abraham. When Abraham was seventy-five years old, God promised to bless him and his descendants (Genesis 12:1-7, 13:16-18). When Abraham was ninety-nine years old, God established His covenant with him giving circumcision as a sign (Genesis 17:1-10). Note and remember that God made a covenant with him and promised to bless Abraham while he was yet uncircumcised.

Earlier scripture, introduces us to the faith expressions of Abraham, who would later be called the "father of faith." From earlier scripture we see that king Chedorlaomer kidnapped Lot, Abraham's nephew, and took all of his possessions (Genesis 14:5-12). Uncle Abraham organized a military expedition, went to war, and regained Lot's freedom and retrieved all of Lot's possessions (Genesis 14:14-16).

Returning from this successful expedition, Abraham met a man named Melchizedek (Genesis 14:18-20). This Melchizedek was king of Salem which is believed to have later become Jerusalem, for Salem meant peace. This man, Melchizedek, was also a priest of God Most High. Note that Melchizedek held both the office of king and the office of priest. No one, other than Jesus Christ Himself, ever succeeded in holding both offices. King Uzziah tried, but was smitten with leprosy for his arrogance (2 Chronicles 26:16-23). During Israel's history, kings descended from the tribe of Judah while the priests descended from the tribe of Levi. But Melchizedek belonged to an order of priesthood unique and far older than the Levitical priesthood, which descended from Aaron, Moses' brother. As king, Melchizedek exercised power with men for God, but as priest, he exercised power with God for men.

Indeed, God had blessed Abraham with a successful military campaign. As Abraham returned from that successful expedition, Melchizedek met him and blessed him. In response to his being blessed, Abraham paid a tenth (tithe) of all his increase to Melchizedek, the priest. At the zenith of his power and influence, Abraham paid a tithe.

Abraham's tithe-paying was his joyous and voluntary response toward God for the victory he had been given. Abraham's tithe was his voluntarily tribute to the greatness of Melchizedek, the priest. Through the tithe, Abraham acknowledged his inferiority and the superiority of the priest, Melchizedek. Abraham expressed his faith by tithing, so the tithe was Abraham's expression of faith.

Later scripture, the New Testament, provides the Holy Spirit's contemporary interpretation and application of God's covenant dealing with Abraham (Hebrews 7:1-10). When Abraham returned from rescuing his nephew, Lot, he enjoyed a blessed encounter with a noteworthy man named Melchizedek. Melchizedek was the priest who also served as king, for in the Hebrew language the name Melchizedek meant king of righteousness (Hebrews 7:2).

Melchizedek had the power to bless man—Jesus has the power to bless man. Because Melchizedek was both king and priest he was a "type" of Christ. Righteousness and peace met in Melchizedek making him a type of Christ. Righteousness and peace results from the atoning and interceding work of the priest. Christ is the antitype of Melchizedek.

It is obvious that the priesthood of Melchizedek is patterned according to the priesthood of Christ. If the priesthood of Melchizedek is patterned according to the priesthood of Christ, are not the blessings of the priesthood of Melchizedek also patterned according to the blessings of the priesthood of Christ?

Again, later scripture presents God's covenant dealing with Abraham as a picturesque portrait for all generations. Abraham is called the *"father of all who believe"* (Romans 4:11), thus Abraham became a "type" of the believer.

Note that before Abraham had been circumcised he became the father of all who believe (Romans 4:10-16). He also became the father of the circumcision and the father of the uncircumcision before he was circumcised. Abraham became the father to those who would follow in his steps of faith, so through faith we are all sons of Abraham (Galatians 3:7). Through Christ, the blessings of the faith contained in the promise made to Abraham come to us (Galatians 3:14).

Faith is what we do instrumentally about what we believe intellectually that which God indeed has approved (2 Corinthians 4:13). First God approves it, we believe it, and then act according to what we believe God approved.

Time and time again, the faith of Abraham is held as a model for us (Romans 4:11-12, 16). Therefore, understanding and imitating the faith expressions of Abraham enhances our spirituality.

God blessed Abraham, the one to whom the promises of faith were given. God delivered the people and spoils into the hand of Abraham, the one to whom the promises of faith were given. Thus, the one to whom the promises of faith were given received an increase.

Abraham, the one to whom the promises of faith were given, received a blessing from God. After receiving the blessing, Abraham, the one to whom the promises of faith were given, paid a tenth (tithe) of all his increase to the priest. Since we share the relationship to Abraham that Christ does to Melchizedek, who could argue against the fact that blessings and tithes are positioned as a pattern for the believers to whom the promises of faith have been given?

Abraham, the one to whom the promises of faith were given, received a "credited" righteousness from God. After receiving a credited righteousness, Abraham became the father of faith for us. Since God credits righteousness and urges us to follow in the steps of the faith of our father Abraham, who could argue against the fact that credited righteousness and tithing are positioned as a pattern for the believers to whom the promises of faith have been given?

Remember that Abraham became the father of the faithful before he was circumcised. Paying tithes was the exercise of faith that Abraham engaged in before he was circumcised. Tithing is the only exercise of faith that is connected with an expressed blessing for Abraham before he was circumcised (Genesis 14:18-20).

GOD'S HONORARIUM—THE PERMANENCE: ABRAHAM

As Abraham's tithe was his voluntary response to God for His blessings, so the tithe is our voluntary response to God for His blessings. We tithe, not because of the commandment of the Law of the Lord, but because of our commitment of love for the Lord. As Abraham's tithe was his way of honoring God's honorarium, the tithe is our way of honoring God's honorarium. Jesus illustrated it best when He said:

> *He who receives you receives Me, and he who receives Me receives Him who sent Me. He who receives a prophet in the name of a prophet shall receive a prophet's reward; and he who receives a righteous man in the name of a righteous man shall receive a righteous man's reward. And whoever in the name of a disciple gives to one of these little ones even a cup of cold water to drink, truly I say to you, he shall not lose his reward.*
> —MATTHEW 10:40-42

▸ God appreciates the choices of His people and appropriates His resources for His people when they act without Him having to command it.

Blessings await those who will simply do what God approves. God appreciates the choices of His people and appropriates His resources for His people when they act without Him having to command it.

When children are immature, parents command, children obey, and parents express their appreciation. For example, parents command children to wash the dishes. Children wash the dishes because they received the command from their parents. Parents express their appreciation for their children's obedience to the command. When children become mature, parents no longer command them to wash the dishes. Children wash the dishes because of their love for their parents and parents still express their appreciation for their children's expression of love.

The immature respond when they receive commands. The mature respond when they receive an opportunity. The immature receive their promised rewards when they respond to the commands they have been given. The mature receive their promised rewards when they respond to the opportunities they have been given. Therefore, for the faithful believer, tithing has nothing to do with command, but has all to do with promise. The question, therefore, is not what will God take away from us if we do not tithe, but what will God add to us if we do tithe? The promise yet stands, *"Now this I say, he who sows sparingly will also reap sparingly, and he who sows bountifully will also reap bountifully"* (2 Corinthians 9:6).

For the precise and concise analytical mind, let's examine the **who.** Melchizedek was made king and priest like the Son of God, Jesus (Hebrews 7:3). Jesus Christ is king and priest according to the order of Melchizedek (Hebrews 7:17). Abraham is the father of faith to all believers (Romans 4:11). We, believers, are counted as the sons of Abraham (Galatians 3:7).

GOD'S HONORARIUM—THE PERMANENCE: ABRAHAM

For the precise and concise analytical mind, let's examine the **what**. God blessed Abraham and Abraham gave a tenth (tithe) of all his increase. God has blessed us. What should we do? Does God expect us to do any differently than our father Abraham? Indeed God expects us to tithe all of our increase just as Abraham's example of faith did. Should we do any differently than our father Abraham? Certainly, we should not. We should walk in the steps of Abraham, our father of faith.

Chapter 23

GOD'S HONORARIUM— THE PROSPERITY: TITHE & OFFERINGS

JESUS COMMENDED THE POOR WIDOW FOR GIVING all she had (Luke 21:1-4); He *commanded* the rich ruler to give all he had (Luke 18:22). God established the system of tithes and offering (Deuteronomy 12:6; 11); we do well to honor God's established system of tithes and offerings.

Tithes are distinctively different from offerings though the terms are occasionally used interchangeably (Deuteronomy 12:6, 11, Malachi 3:8, 2 Chronicles 31:12, Nehemiah 13:5). The tithe was a system specifically regulated by heaven as a

GOD'S HONORARIUM—THE PROSPERITY: TITHE & OFFERINGS

percentage, ten percent (Leviticus 27:30-32). Heaven regulated it as a priority because it was the first tenth (Deuteronomy 26:1-10; Genesis 4:4). The offering was a system categorically regulated by the heart (Exodus 35:4, 21, 26, 29).

The tithing system was honored before the Law of Moses (Genesis 14:18-20, 28:20-22) and Jesus honored the system of tithing (Luke 11:42, Matthew 23:23).

God uses His system of tithes and offerings to get good things to His people. When we honor Him with our tithe, God increases our income (Malachi 3:10) and decreases our expenses (Malachi 3:11). What we give determines what we receive (Luke 6:38).

When Solomon spoke with God, he reminisced about how God had granted generational favors to his family, *"Solomon said to God, 'You have dealt with my father David with great lovingkindness, and have made me king in his place. Now, O LORD God, Your promise to my father David is fulfilled, for You have made me king over a people as numerous as the dust of the earth'"* (2 Chronicles 1:8-9). Therefore, with confidence, Solomon asked God for wisdom and knowledge, *"Give me now wisdom and knowledge, that I may go out and come in before this people, for who can rule this great people of Yours?"* (2 Chronicles 1:10).

When God spoke with King Solomon, He granted the king abundant wisdom so that he became the wisest man to ever live. Though Solomon did not ask for it, God granted him wealth so that he became the wealthiest man to ever live:

God said to Solomon, "Because you had this in mind, and did not ask for riches, wealth or honor, or the life of those who hate you, nor have you even asked for long life, but you have asked for yourself wisdom and knowledge that you may rule My people over whom I have made you king, wisdom and knowledge have been granted to you. And I will give you riches and wealth and honor, such as none of the kings who were before you has possessed nor those who will come after you"

—2 Chronicles 1:11-12

Would you like for God to respond to you in such manner? Would you like for God to give you more than you ask for? Are you willing to respond to God the way Solomon responded to God and receive the same response?

How did Solomon respond? Just exactly what triggered such an outpouring of wisdom and wealth?

Notice the time of the response, *"In that night God appeared to Solomon and said to him, 'Ask what I shall give you'"* (2 Chronicles 1:7). What had happened in that night or just prior to that night? *"Solomon went up there before the LORD to the bronze altar which was at the tent of meeting, and offered a thousand burnt offerings on it"* (2 Chronicles 1:7). The night after Solomon had given a great sacrificial offering to God, God gave a great offering to Solomon.

Ezra proclaimed a fast (Ezra 8:21-23) and then gave an unsolicited offering invoking the favor of God (Ezra 8:24-30). God then delivered them safely (Ezra 8:31). Gifts to God attract greater gifts from God.

GOD'S HONORARIUM—THE PROSPERITY: TITHE & OFFERINGS

In his first letter to the Corinthians, Paul requested a collection from the Corinthian believers (1 Corinthians 16:1-2). Though this was a monetary collection, he never referred to it as a financial offering. Instead, Paul called it a grace of God (8:1), gracious work (8:7, 19), proof of love and reason for boasting (8:24), ministry to the saints (9:1), and ministry of service (9:12) contrasting this ministry to the sowing of seed.

When we sow a little we will reap a little, *"...he who sows sparingly will also reap sparingly..."* (2 Corinthians 9:6a). If we sow one apple seed we limit ourselves to one apple tree. When we limit ourselves to one apple tree we also limit ourselves to reaping the fruit from only one apple tree.

Likewise, when we sow much we will reap much, *"...he who sows bountifully will also reap bountifully"* (2 Corinthians 9:6b). If we sow one-hundred apple seeds we increase ourselves to one-hundred apple trees. When we increase ourselves to one-hundred apple trees we also increase ourselves to reaping the fruit from one-hundred apple trees.

The first portion of God's blessing is for sowing while the next portion of God's blessing is for consuming, *"Now He who supplies seed to the sower and bread for food will supply and multiply your seed for sowing and increase the harvest of your righteousness"* (2 Corinthians 9:10). God gives a specific seed for us to sow and He gives a specific portion for us to consume (Isaiah 55:10).

Jesus ordered the rich ruler to give his financial resources to the poor (Luke 18:22). He was not trying to take money away from the rich ruler, but instead was trying to get money to the rich ruler (Luke 18:28-28). Jesus may have been requesting a contribution into His treasury of which Judas held custody. From His treasury, Jesus regularly gave to the poor out of His financial resources (John 13:29; 12:5).

Some have argued that tithing was confined to and implemented to be strictly an Old Testament Law. They usually argue that 1 Corinthians 16 is the foundational principle for new covenant givers. Let's examine the validity of this assertion.

The apostle Paul ordered the churches in Galatia and the church in Corinth to set aside monies the first day of each week (1 Corinthians 16:1-2). Paul's perception of the deep poverty of the Macedonians may have caused him to exempt them from giving. Nevertheless, *"… of their own accord"* (1 Corinthians 8:3) they begged for the opportunity to participate, *"begging us with much urging for the favor of participation in the support of the saints"* (2 Corinthians 8:4). Therefore, if 1 Corinthians 16:1 is the basis for the new covenant worshipper to give, what was the basis for the Macedonians?

Some have abused while others have refused the concept of tithing, but tithing is so important that it deserves a repeated emphasis. God established the system of tithes and offerings. Tithes are distinguishably different from offerings in that tithes are specifically regulated by heaven as the first ten percent, while offerings are regulated by the heart. Tithing existed before the Law of Moses, but was honored by

Jesus. Those who withheld their tithe robbed God and were punished. God rewarded those who paid their tithe.

> You establish the size of your harvest when you plant; what and where you plant determines what you reap. Sow to your harvest size not *from* your harvest size.

Furthermore, God uses the system of tithes and offerings to get good things to His people. You establish the size of your harvest when you plant; what and where you plant determines what you reap. Sow **to** your harvest size not *from* your harvest size. God multiplies what you sow (plant) not what you harvest and eat (keep). God multiples what you sow in order for you to have all sufficiency in everything for yourself and for others (2 Corinthians 9:8). God's recommended way to increase is not by investing in stocks and bonds, but within ministry (Luke 6:38, Proverbs 11:25). Give promptly and consistently of each increase.

Chapter 24

GOD'S STEWARDSHIP— ATTITUDES AND BLESSINGS

GOD CALLS EACH DISCIPLE TO BECOME A STEWARD. Stewards use their God-given abilities to manage their God-given resources to accomplish God's intended results (1 Corinthians 4:1-7; Colossians 1:25, 1 Peter 4:10). Stewards manage their finances by their faith.

ATTITUDES (LUKE 10:25-37)

Time and time again, scripture defines a steward as one who is a faithful disciple. To be faithful is to fulfill assigned responsibility. The apostle Paul sent Tychicus to make known to the Ephesians how he was doing. Paul considered him to be faithful because he would fulfill that assignment (Ephesians 6:21-22, Colossians 4:7-9). Indeed, it is necessary for a steward to be trustworthy and faithful (1 Corinthians 4:1-2).

God calls stewards to manage their financial resources by faith (Luke 10:25-37). How can one improve his stewardship? The story of the "Good Samaritan" helps us to consider the attitudes involved in stewardship development.

- The robber's attitude was one of, "What is yours is mine and I am going to get it" (Luke 10:30). He thought that he should have whatever belonged to others. We want nothing to do with those who attack others within the physical realm, but many keep company with those who do so in the spiritual realm.

- Excessive taxation revolves upon the principle of unjustly taking what rightfully belongs to others (Romans 13:6). Lotteries revolve upon the principle of taking unfairly what rightfully belongs to others (Ephesians 4:28).

- The priest and Levite's attitude was, "What is mine is mine and I am going to keep it" (Luke 10:31-32). They thought they should hoard everything God had given to them. We kind of like this attitude and justify it by saying, "They took nothing that did not belong to them therefore they have hurt no one."

- The priest and Levite were like those who picnic in the park and when finished, remove the table cloth, put the trash away, and take the extra food with them. They do not consider that someone else had planted the trees for shade and built the table for their comfort. Therefore, they never thought to replenish for the next generation. No doubt they felt they were too busy with their time. No doubt they felt they were too poor.

- The Samaritan's attitude was one of, "What is mine is yours and I am going to give it" (Luke 10:33-37). He saw himself as one who was only a steward of the resources that God had put at his disposal, and that he should share with his neighbor. We like this man as long as no one asks us to imitate him as he gave his time and his money.

Let us observe some similarities. They each saw the same need, and likely were pursuing some task when they saw the victim. All could have offered excuses. The priest and Levite could have offered a theological excuse. After all, they were on a ministry mission. The Samaritan could have offered a social excuse. After all, everyone knew that the Jews considered the Samaritans to be outcasts.

Let us consider some differences. This question will help expose the attitude of the robber according to 1 Corinthians 10:26: "If you earned $500 this week, how much of it belongs to God?" Contrast the attitude of priest and Levite with that of the Samaritan, who knew that God gives tomorrow based on what we give today (Matthew 25:23).

Become an active giver today. What are you now enjoying that you did not help to build? What are you now enjoying that you did not develop? What are you leaving for the next generation (1 Peter 1:10-12; 2 Peter 1:15)?

Blessings (1 Chronicles 29:10-16)

Though he ruled over all of Israel for forty years, King David recognized that he was just a steward (1 Chronicles 29:26-27). As a steward, he exercised temporary custody over the resources of God (1 Chronicles 29:15), using his God-given abilities to manage his God-given resources to accomplish God-intended results.

We are stewards as well; therefore, how can we improve our stewardship?

Acknowledging the source of blessings enables us to improve our stewardship. To be blessed is to be positioned for prosperity. To be positioned for prosperity is to have people and circumstances favorably synchronized on our behalf. The lame man had not been blessed with a healing

(John 5:1-9) because when the water was moved, no one was present to put him in the water. When someone was there to put him in the water, it had not been stirred.

God is the source of all of our blessings; He possesses the power to give us all that we need. The earlier scriptures document this in 1 Chronicles 29:11-12, 14, 26-28, 25, while the later scriptures document this in 1 Corinthians 4:7.

God is the source of all of His own blessings, possessing the passion to give to Himself all that He needs. The earlier scriptures document this in 1 Chronicles 29:14, 16, while the later scriptures document this in 2 Corinthians 9:6, 8-15. Those who give, always have the means to give (Luke 6:38).

A father bought his son an order of McDonald's French fries. While the son was eating, the father reached to take two fries for himself. The son withdrew and sternly said, "No!" The father persisted, but the son emphatically said, "No." The father then thought: "Does my son not know that..."

- I am the reason he has fries?
- I could take his fries?
- I could buy myself fries?
- I could buy enough fries to bury him?
- I really do not like fries?
- I really do not need fries?
- All I want is my son's willingness to share with me what I have shared with him?

GOD'S STEWARDSHIP—ATTITUDES AND BLESSINGS

Could it be that those who have not are lacking because they do not give? Should we pray for those who have none to give?

God blesses us so that we can bless Him (1 Chronicles 29:14). He requires of us only of that which He has previously given to us. God blesses us so that we can bless others. He requires of us only of that which He has previously given to us. Children are blessed through the spiritual aptitude of their parents.

Chapter 25

GOD'S STEWARDSHIP—CONTRIBUTION AND EXPECTATIONS

A MORAL-MANNERED RICH MAN ASKED JESUS, *"What shall I do to inherit eternal life?"* Jesus questioned the rich man's motive for his greeting and then directed his attention to the commandments. This rich man claimed to have kept all of the commandments from his youth up, so Jesus gave him a stewardship test, which he failed.

GOD'S STEWARDSHIP—CONTRIBUTION AND EXPECTATIONS

CONTRIBUTION (MARK 10:17-31)

Remember, stewards use their God-given abilities to manage their God-given resources to accomplish God-intended results.

> Good stewards realize that they are just temporary custodial managers over the resources of another.

Good stewards realize that they are just temporary custodial managers over the resources of another. For failing to become a good steward, this man remained spiritually unfulfilled. Likewise, refusing to become a good steward leaves us spiritually unfulfilled.

How can we become good stewards? Consider these radical therapies necessary to become a good steward:

- **Separate yourself from all that prevents your spiritual fulfillment.** Jesus ordered the wealthy young man to invest his resources into the kingdom work of God (Mark 10:21). If he had done so, he would have received a great **earthly** reward (Mark 10:28-30, Matthew 25:14-29).

- **Saturate yourself with all that promotes your spiritual fulfillment.** Jesus ordered the man to invest himself into the kingdom work of God, *"...come, follow Me"* (Mark 10:21). If he had done so, the young man would have received a great **eternal** reward (Mark 10:28-30, Matthew 25:31-46).

What do you have (or what *has* you) that prevents your spiritual fulfillment? Is it the third job that keeps you from Bible study, worship, fellowship, prayer, and spiritual meditation? Why do you have a third job? Is it to pay for the fourth TV? Why do you need a fourth TV? So that you will have something to put in your fifth bedroom so your sixth cousins will have something to watch every seventh month when they come to visit?

Sometimes religious people need radical therapy. Instead of giving $2 give $200 or even $2,000! Do something radically generous today.

Expectations (Luke 6:20-38)

We must become good stewards. How can we become good stewards? Let us consider these revolutionary truths.

- ▸ **Be more than you are expected to be.** You are not expected to be happy when circumstances are unfavorable, so be happy regardless of the circumstance.

GOD'S STEWARDSHIP—CONTRIBUTION AND EXPECTATIONS

- **Be happy when you are without finances** (Luke 6:20-21), even when you have no mortgage payment or no money for new sneakers.

- **Be happy when you are without friends** (Luke 6:22-23). Stand alone at work or at school. At the time, those without were investors (contributors). Investors increased. At the time, those with were consumers. Consumers decreased (Matthew 25:14-30).

- **Do more than you are expected to do.** You are not expected to do good when circumstances are unfavorable, so do good regardless of circumstances.

- **Do good to your enemies** (Luke 6:27-30, 32). Help unfavorable coworkers and classmates.

- **Do good when your finances will not be replaced** (Luke 6:33-35). Help your coworkers and fellow students who are unable to repay.

OBSERVATIONS

- Those who give, receive (Luke 6:23, 35) and their receipts are based upon their gifts (Luke 6:38).

- Many unacceptable excuses surface. "If I had assets I would give." How many assets do you need in order to love others, pray for others, and speak well of enemies?

- God doesn't expect you to give that much. Who are you fooling? God wants you to give beyond human expectation.

Chapter 26

GOD'S STEWARDSHIP— WATCHING THE WISDOM OF A WIDOW WOMAN

JESUS EVALUATED HOW BOTH THE RICH AND POOR gave their financial contribution. To His disciples, He reported His findings and had them recorded for us to know (Luke 21:1-4). Thus, we see that giving is a personal matter but not a private matter.

We must evaluate our own personal financial contribution in order to know what percentage of God's money we are keeping and/or spending for ourselves (family). Jesus said that the widow woman had contributed more than all the other contributors (Luke 21:3). Did she give more in total amount? No! But she had given a greater percentage for she had given 100 percent. For example: Disciple A has $500 and contributes $100 (20%). Disciple B has $1,000 and contributes $150 (15%). Who has given more?

In what way had the widow given more? By giving 100% she had nothing left. For example: Disciple A has $500, contributes $100 and has $400 left. Disciple B has $1,000, contributes $400 and has $600 left. Who has more money left?

In an effort to deny that God concerns himself with amount, some have argued that a little given with the proper attitude is better than much given with an improper attitude. I suggest giving much with the proper attitude. Nothing in this text addresses attitude and never suggests that the rich had improper attitudes. This text addresses **amount**.

To determine the percentage of your gross income you are keeping and/or spending for yourself, divide total monthly contribution by total monthly income. To determine the total amount of your gross income that you are keeping and/or spending for yourself, subtract total monthly contribution from total monthly income.

"… *remember the words of the Lord Jesus, that He Himself said, 'It is more blessed to give than to receive'*" (Acts 20:35).

God required His people to always assemble with an offering for Him. As a matter of fact, His people were never to come before Him empty-handed (Exodus 23:15, 34:20,

Deuteronomy 16:16). Because of their willingness to give, God blessed them bountifully.

Likewise, we should get in the habit of bringing the Lord a gift every time we come together. What a way to celebrate the goodness of God at every assembly, *"Give, and it will be given to you. They will pour into your lap a good measure pressed down, shaken together, and running over. For by your standard of measure it will be measured to you in return"* (Luke 6:38). Do you trust God enough to try Him?

Chapter 27

FAMILY FINANCIAL MODELS

THE QUALITY OF FINANCIAL MANAGEMENT IS MORE important than the quantity of income. Remember, millionaires go broke, too, so families need financial models.

When there is only one income producer and one spender, money management is strictly economical. But when there are two, money management is both economical and emotional. Therefore, each husband and wife needs to establish a financial model. It is not only crucial to receive enough money, but to disburse it in a manner that is acceptable to both you and your spouse. Numerous sound financial models exist, so use one that accommodates you and your spouse's income, expenditures and dispositions. In the event the model fails to adequately accommodate both of you, adjust it or adopt another one that will.

MODELS

1. One spouse pays all the expenditures for the entire family, while the other spouse accountably saves and invests his/her total income.

2. One spouse pays all the expenditures for the entire family, while the other spouse accountably saves and invests a portion of his/her income.

3. One spouse pays all the expenditures for the entire family, while the other spouse unaccountably spends.

4. One spouse assumes responsibility for scheduled and recurring expenditures, while one spouse assumes responsibility for accidental, incidental and non-recurring expenditures.

5. Family expenditures are divided into two categories, each spouse assumes total responsibility for one category.

6. All income is deposited into one account. One spouse maintains custody. All expenditures are governed by the jurisdiction of that custodial spouse.

7. All income is deposited into one account. Both husband and wife corroborate expenditures.

8. All income is deposited into one account. Husband and wife corroborate expenditures that exceed a preset spending limit.

9. All income is deposited into one account. Husband and wife designate certain categories of expenses to be paid automatically, but corroborate every other expenditure.

10. Each spouse retains an agreed upon percentage or amount of his/her income to keep for personal designated items,. All remaining income is jointly held and allocated only after corroboration of both husband and wife.

Epilogue

Thanks for reading through to the final pages of this book. All along, I have been praying that you would feel the rising urge of the surge of God within your soul.

Though the uncertainties around us provide much ambiguity, the God within us anchors our hearts and soul, "...for He Himself has said, "I WILL NEVER DESERT YOU, NOR WILL I EVER FORSAKE, YOU,' so that we confidently say, 'THE LORD IS MY HELPER, I WILL NOT BE AFRAID. WHAT WILL MAN DO TO ME?" (Hebrews 13:5-6). Indeed it is true, a better you begins with a grace view of God. Therefore, we should continue to "Let the glory of the Lord rise among us."

Other books by John Marshall

Good and Angry
A Personal Guide to Anger Management

God Knows!
There Is No Need to Worry

God, Listen!
Prayers That God Always Answers
(includes addiction-recovery guide)

Final Answer
You Asked, God Answered

My God!
Who He Is Will Change Your Life

The Power of the Tongue
What You Say Is What You Get

Success Is a God Idea

Show Me the Money
7 Exercises That Build Economic Strength

Faith, Family & Finances—Volume Two
A Practical Message to Get Us Out of the Painful Mess We Are In

Contact Information

John Marshall
P.O. Box 2136
Stone Mountain GA 30086,
(404) 297.9050
jdm@graceview.us

www.ingramcontent.com/pod-product-compliance
Lightning Source LLC
Chambersburg PA
CBHW051433290426
44109CB00016B/1541